Other histories

Other Histories explores the nature of history and assesses the position of history within social anthropology. In recent years the historical dimension of other cultures has become an integrated part of any anthropological inquiry, while the different ways of producing history have themselves become a sphere of interest within anthropology itself.

Using historical and ethnographic material, the contributors to this book focus on the historical scene in Europe to show how cultural concepts act as forces of historical causation. They establish a radically new view of history itself by analyzing what has previously been seen as the unity and progress of European history. They demonstrate that history is not linear but highly complex, often containing several separate local histories, and they emphasize the interdependence of culture and history, showing clearly that there is no way of separating structure and change.

Kirsten Hastrup is Professor of Anthropology at the University of Copenhagen.

EUROPEAN ASSOCIATION OF SOCIAL ANTHROPOLOGISTS

The European Association of Social Anthropologists (EASA) was inaugurated in January 1989, in response to a widely-felt need for a professional association which would represent social anthropologists in Europe, and foster co-operation and interchange in teaching and research. As Europe transforms itself in the 1990s, the EASA is dedicated to the renewal of the distinctive European tradition in social anthropology.

Other titles in the series

Conceptualizing society
Adam Kuper

Revitalizing European rituals
Jeremy Boissevain

Alcohol, gender and culture
Dimitra Gefou-Madianou

Understanding rituals
Daniel de Coppet

Other histories

Edited by
Kirsten Hastrup

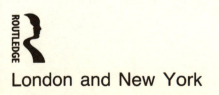

London and New York

First published 1992
by Routledge
11 New Fetter Lane, London EC4P 4EE

Simultaneously published in the USA and Canada
by Routledge
a division of Routledge, Chapman and Hall, Inc.
29 West 35th Street, New York, NY 10001

Phototypeset in 10 on 12 pt Times by Intype, London
Printed and bound in Great Britain by
Biddles Ltd, Guildford and King's Lynn

British Library Cataloguing in Publication Data
A catalogue record for this book is available from the
British Library.

Library of Congress Cataloguing in Publication Data
Other histories/edited by Kirsten Hastrup.
   p.   cm.
   'A Collection of papers from the first conference of the newly
formed European Association of Social Anthropologists.'
Includes bibliographical references and index.
   1. History—Philosophy—Congresses. 2. Europe—History—
Philosophy—Congresses. 3. History—Methodology—Congresses.
4. Anthropology—Congresses. I. Hastrup, Kirsten. II. European
Association of Social Anthropologists.
   D16.8.O815   1992
   901—dc20   92–984
                                       CIP

ISBN 0–415–06122–9
     0–415–06123–7 (pbk)

Contents

Contributors

Anton Blok is Professor of Cultural Anthropology at the University of Amsterdam. He has done extensive fieldwork in Sicily and archival work in the Netherlands. His publications include *The Mafia of a Sicilian Village* (Cambridge, 1988) and *De Bokkeryders* (Amsterdam, 1991).

John Davis is Professor of Social Anthropology at Oxford University. He has done fieldwork in Italy and Libya. His publications include *Libyan Politics: Tribe and Revolution* (London, 1987) and *Exchange* (Open University Press, 1992).

Kirsten Hastrup is Professor of Anthropology at the University of Copenhagen. She has done fieldwork and historical research in Iceland. Her publications include *Nature and Policy in Iceland 1400–1800: An Anthropological Analysis of History and Mentality* (Oxford, 1990) and *Island of Anthropology: Studies in Icelandic Past and Present* (Odense, 1990).

Thomas Hauschild is Professor of Anthropology at the University of Tübingen. He has done extensive fieldwork in southern Italy. His publications include *Der Böse Blick: Ideengeschichtliche und sozialpsychologische Untersuchungen* (Berlin, 1992).

Michael Herzfeld is Professor of Anthropology at Harvard University. He has done extensive fieldwork on Crete and has also worked in the Dodecanese. His publications include *A Place in History: Social and Monumental Time in a Cretan Town* (Princeton, 1991) and *The Social Production of Indifference: Exploring the Symbolic Roots of Western Bureaucracy* (Oxford, 1992).

Anne Knudsen is a Senior Research Fellow in Anthropology at the University of Copenhagen. She has done fieldwork and archival studies in Corsica. Her monograph on the historical anthropology of Corsica will appear in English as *An Island in History*.

João de Pina-Cabral is Research Fellow at the Institute of Social Sciences at the University of Lisbon. He has carried out fieldwork in northwestern Portugal and among the Eurasian population of Macao. His publications include *Sons of Adam, Daughters of Eve* (Oxford, 1986), and *Os Contextos da Antropologia* (Lisbon, 1991).

Introduction

Kirsten Hastrup

When the making of history was chosen as one of the topics for the first conference of the European Association of Social Anthropologists in Coimbra in 1990, the idea was to provide a coherent picture of the position of 'history' in social anthropology after a number of years of apparently successful attempts at 'historicizing' the discipline. The growing awareness of history had entailed a greater concern with time and change in society, and it had also meant an increasing sensitivity towards different modes of producing and thinking about history in different societies. After renewed reflection on those 'Other Cultures' that Beattie (1964) had claimed to be the object of anthropology, we had come to realize that the range of 'otherness' also incorporated a vast number of separate histories. The discovery of the territory of historical anthropology, which for a decade had been the arena of creative exchange between students of history and students of anthropology (Löfgren 1987), had gradually led to a redefinition of the distinctly anthropological object.

Other Histories is offered as a set of reflections upon the nature of history – including a questioning of our own concepts of history in the light of other histories. As it happens, most of the chapters in this volume draw upon European material, demonstrating the inherent plurality of history in Europe. Thus the apparently Eurocentric vision has the paradoxical effect of breaking down modern European history's alleged uniqueness and unity.

A particular Western sense of history has been defined as a mode of consciousness which assumes social change to be homogeneous, continuous, and linear (Lévi-Strauss 1966). Concern with an understanding of the uniqueness of the European experience has been the *leit-motif* of social philosophy since the eighteenth century (Rowlands 1987: 63). In anthropology 'the others' have been excluded from 'our' history and placed in an altogether different time (Fabian 1983). While possibly entertaining different concepts of time, evidently no society is outside history, as Wolf (1982) has abundantly demonstrated. Peoples outside Europe and of quite different social make-ups were driven to take part in the construction of a common world through the European expansionist policy. While one can sympathize with the project of showing how others became implicated in European history, one would perhaps hesitate to accept that the 'global processes set in motion by European expansion constitute *their* history as well' (Wolf 1982: 385). 'They' should not be admitted to history only by being implicated in ours; they should be allowed their own. As John Davis shows in this volume, there has always been a history without Europe.

[margin note: Not all histories are moved by Europe]

What is more, as can be seen from most of the chapters that follow, the uniqueness and the unity of European history must be dismantled. The unified sense of history seems to be a discursive rather than a social fact and the product of a highly literate Enlightenment heritage. In Europe as elsewhere there is a multiplicity of histories. If our cultural consciousness has become objectified in a particular historical *genre* (cf. Sahlins 1985: 52) that is linearized and continuous, analysis reveals the non-synchronicity and discontinuity of social experience. Anne Knudsen's discussion of the dual nature of Corsican history is a case in point; while certainly implicated in the 'larger' progressive history of Europe, the Corsicans also lived in a quite different historical space. This space was defined not by 'traditional stability' (as opposed to 'modern progress') but by a permanent instability that created its own nerve-racking history of recurrent violence.

Even in present-day Europe, the duality or multiplicity of history cannot be overlooked. Far from creating a homogeneous sense of history, the complexity of European societies has sustained a number of coexisting histories. As is demonstrated by João de Pina-Cabral, our concept of modernity needs urgent revision in the light of the 'pagan survivals' in Europe that defy our notions of unified progress. The Portuguese case shows us that it is the metaphors carrying the élitist or literary historical *genre*, not popular interpretations of history, that have become obsolete. This point is further substantiated by Thomas Hauschild in his chapter on the making of history in southern Italy. During fieldwork, Hauschild experienced how local concepts of tradition worked themselves into what seemed to be a revitaliz- ation of ancient rituals but in fact had little bearing on actual history. In the words of Michael Herzfeld, 'the division between religious tradition and secular modernity is discursive rather than practical'. In the social life of people, tradition and change are two sides of the same coin, not separate entities with distinct historicities.

Generally, when anthropologists bring other histories to the fore, the dominant conventions of historical representation are questioned and the uniqueness of Europe is replaced by a blur- ring of *genres*. Anthropology's specific contribution to the study of history seems to be precisely this: to rewrite world history as a non-domesticated multiple history (cf. Harbsmeier 1989). Although 'theoretically predisposed to emphasize whatever is systematic at the expense of what isn't' (Shweder 1984: 19–20), anthropologists have unearthed enough evidence for the non- coherence of the world – in spite of obvious processes of globaliz- ation – to rewrite its history.

SOCIAL SCIENCES AND HISTORY: A RECONCILIATION

If anything distinguishes European social anthropology it is a concern about social structures. Recently, this legacy from Durk- heim has incorporated also the structures of the *longue durée* and of history in general. This provides a new platform for a theory of history informed by anthropological insight. In the words of Sahlins, this entails an explosion of the concept of history by the anthropological experience of culture (1985: 72). The force of this position is put in perspective by the fact that 'a theory of history has long eluded social anthropology' (Ard- ener 1989: 22) and conversely that 'the historian can be seen as not being sufficiently attentive to social signs and symbols, to constant underlying social functions' (Braudel 1980: 71).

The apparent professional imperatives and exclusions are more often than not the result of institutional accidents. Certainly, the division between history and the social sciences cannot be explained by reference to the empirical; at this level, the historian of today is bound to realize that 'the past is a foreign country' (Lowenthal 1985), and the archaeologist who is left with the material traces of earlier histories may extend his analysis vastly by admitting that artefacts are indeed 'symbols in action' (Hodder 1982). Therefore, the often noted allegation that history is concerned with 'facts' and social science with 'theory' (Jones 1976) can no longer be maintained.

It is in the nature of social anthropology to deal with wholes. Since the invention of fieldwork, the whole has generally been conceived of as a local culture, forming an 'island of anthropology' (Hastrup 1990a; 1990b). Such islands have been studied mainly from a synchronic perspective – partly because the first societies to be subjected to this new method of study were societies without written records, partly because the distinctive aim of social anthropology in the Durkheimian tradition was to conceptualize the social system in terms of its internal functional coherence. This trend was largely a reaction to the dominant historicist trends of nineteenth-century scholarship in the humanities; whatever its origin, however, one of its consequences was a remarkable estrangement of social anthropology and history in this century (Chapman *et al.* 1989: 3). Even where 'historical records' existed they were often ignored by social anthropologists, allegedly blocked by 'presentism' (Peel 1989: 200). Whether we accept this label or not, it is true that social anthropology first tended to ignore change as an inherent feature of all societies and, next – when it became all too apparent that societies were manifestly changing – split reality in two and made theories of stability, on the one hand, theories of change, on the other (Chapman *et al.* 1989: 4).

No less unfortunate was the hierarchization of structure and change. The implicit notions of stability as constitutional and change as accidental made early anthropologists go for the 'real' stuff of structure, wholeness, and coherence. Social change was seen as fit work for the second-rate: 'Malinowski sent me to study social change because, he said, I didn't know enough anthropology for fieldwork of the standard type' (Mair 1969: 8). This asymmetrical relationship between studies of social structure and studies of social change was correlated with a view of the real fieldworker as completely detached from the society under study while the downgraded 'applied anthropologist' not only studied but actively induced change. Today we know that no ethnographer can record uncontaminated evidence about social structure: 'The observer is *always* a key part of the *changing* scene that he/she observes' (Leach 1989: 39). As subtly qualified by a range of recent ethnographies, our present epistemological awareness has forced us to admit that 'traditional' culture or society is simply not available for inspection.

Recent studies of particular histories have made it abundantly clear that the separation of structure and history, stability and change is wholly arbitrary (see, e.g., Sahlins 1985; Hastrup 1985; 1990a; Knudsen 1989). All histories are grounded in structures – systematic orderings of contingent circumstances (Sahlins 1985: 144). In their turn, such structures become manifest only through historical events conflating past and present by bringing together 'movements of different origins, of a different rhythm: today's time dates from yesterday, the day before yesterday, and all former times' (Braudel 1980: 34).

In other words, anthropologists have realized that culture and history are adjective to one another (Hastrup 1985: 246), not substantially separated entities. Metaphor and reality merge and set society in motion (Sahlins 1981). The historicizing of the islands of anthropology has implied a theoretical reconciliation of stability and change; whereas before anthropologists tended to confuse history and change, we have now come to realize that stability is no less 'historical' than rapid movement (Sahlins 1985: 144).

If the marriage between history and social anthropology today seems a happy one, the period of courtship has been long and has had its temporary setbacks. As early as 1899 the legal historian Maitland ventured the point that 'by and by anthropology will have the choice between being history and being nothing' (Maitland 1936 [1899]: 249). His target was the then-dominant evolutionist paradigm which modelled anthropology on the natural sciences. While the mould disintegrated, the illusion of 'primitive society' persisted in shaping the anthropological object (Kuper 1988). In spite of the fierceness of Maitland's proclamation, the fields of history and anthropology were not immediately engaged; on the face of it, anthropology chose to be 'nothing'.

This 'nothingness' gave birth, however, to another non-evolutionary approach. With fieldwork as its empirical base and Durkheim's 'rules' as its theoretical foundation, social anthropology became increasingly concerned with the systematics of society as an essentially non-temporal entity. Again, this led to a serious flirtation with the natural sciences that peaked with Radcliffe-Brown's claim that social anthropology aims at isolating the natural laws of society. Evans-Pritchard's famous statement from 1950 that fundamentally 'social anthropology is a kind of historiography' (Evans-Pritchard 1964: 152) was a reaction to this and a reclaiming of social anthropology for the humanities. The switch from function to meaning which followed from this was soon accomplished but without any serious impact on the anthropological concern with history. The claim made by Dumont that 'history is the movement by which society reveals itself as what it is' (quoted by Evans-Pritchard 1964: 182) led to little more than a renewed interest in *society* as a bounded whole. Evans-Pritchard himself implicitly emphasized this in the discussion following his claim that anthropology must be a kind of historiography: when dealing with the development of a social system, 'do we then speak of a society at different points in time or do we speak of [two] different societies?' (Evans-Pritchard 1964: 181). The relevant question still concerns 'society' – reflecting the current definition of the analytical object of anthropology.

It was not until the appearance in 1968 of *History and Social Anthropology* that history as such became conspicuous. While many anthropologists had already dealt with historical records at the time, and while both the German and the American tradition of anthropology had been explicitly historical, it was the Association of Social Anthropologists volume edited by Lewis (1968) that finally placed history on the agenda of British anthropology. However, it was 'history' in the limited sense of the past and largely identified with historical records. The small conjunctive 'and' gives away the game. There was no integration of the two subjects, only additive information about society owing to the longer time perspective. In his introduction, Lewis maintains that 'history remains essentially a way of looking at data, and of asking and answering the question "Why?" in relation to specific occurrences' (p. x). The implicit notion of 'temporal causation' has a distinct tradition in European scholarship, where causes have generally been identified as antecedents. As I have shown in the case of Iceland, this view of causation is essentially non-anthropological.

Since then, things have moved fast in social anthropology. The 'historical anthropology' of the late seventies and the eighties eventually succeeded in integrating the fields of history and social science – to the extent that we no longer need to speak of historical anthropology because social anthropology as a whole has become historicized. The analytical object has been redefined.

THE ANALYTICAL OBJECT

As is implied by the quotation from Evans-Pritchard above, we have tended to define our object of study in spatial terms. We have dealt with societies and cultures as entities separated from one another in space. By contrast, historians have dealt with periods or epochs. A truly 'historical' anthropology must include reference to both space and time, not only because 'history' is the unfolding of society through time but also because 'society' is the institutional form of historical events (Sahlins 1985: xii). The merging of society and history in the anthropological object defines this as 'a state' – that is, a condition that obtains in a particular time-space. The objective condition is matched by a subjective reality, a world of experience, in which time is always part of the definition of the present. It is this world that we enter during fieldwork, discovering and defining it at the same time (Hastrup 1987a; 1987b).

In contrast to earlier views of traditional societies, there is no inherent claim to either the stability or the structural coherence of the 'world'. Discursive integration may mask actual disjunctions within a particular social space. In this vein, Robert Paine has recently argued, for instance, that 'there is more than one "time", and more than one "place", in the space that is Israel, among the Jews in Israel today' (Paine 1989: 127–8). In order to understand the complexity of 'modern' histories we must take such disjunctions into account. In his chapter on segmentation in Greece, Michael Herzfeld also demonstrates how even a unified historical narrative may provide the means of creating opposite interpretations which in turn sustain political rivalry in the local community.

'Worlds' can be seen as self-defining social spaces within which particular realities are generated, regenerated, or transformed through social practice. 'Events' are registered and defined as such not by their objective properties but by their significance in terms of a particular cultural scheme (Sahlins 1985; Hastrup 1987b). In other words, events are happenings of social signifi-

events

cance; that is how they are registered as events in the first place and distinguished from the motley and continuous mass of mere happenings. This also implies that particular happenings which from the outside appear to be of some moment for the social system under consideration may fail to register as events in local terms. This 'failure' seems to have contributed to the dissolution of Icelandic society in the sixteenth to eighteenth centuries. If practical interest is symbolically constituted (Sahlins 1976: 207), the evidence from Iceland suggests that practical interest may be constituted by an anachronistic symbolic scheme, the result being a disintegration of the social system.

We must be careful here not to imagine arrows of causation from symbolic or cultural schemes to the material situation. Rather than causing each other, conceptual and material realities are simultaneous (Ardener 1982: 6). Culture is an implication from action and speech events, and any interpretation of a particular reality must begin with the source of simultaneities, dissolving the familiar opposition between idealism and materialism (p. 11).

In the present connection this implies a problem of separating discourse from reality, 'tradition' from 'history'. The two merge in the (re)storing of identity, as Paine has shown. In the effort to heighten Jewish self-awareness through a restoration of tradition, it appears that 'much of this activity is a striving "to rebecome what they never were" ' (1989: 131). The paradox, which draws upon Schechner's (1981) concept of restored behaviour, was noted also by Hauschild in his witnessing of revitalized rituals in southern Italy. Images of 'self' work their way into historical events, a point which is also aptly illustrated by Herzfeld's study of the world of the Greeks. While all actors seem to agree *structurally* to a unified historical narrative, they disagree radically about its *realization in specific events*. Political stands and the corresponding notions of the acting selves make people live in different plot-spaces. This living in different plot-spaces within one world may be the result not only of factionalism but also of a different kind of power game in which, as Pina-Cabral shows, the Church may play a crucial role.

Worlds have their own modes of producing history and their own ways of thinking about it. These two aspects of any history are closely interwoven. Davis reminds us that the irreversible is not necessarily the inevitable but the outcome of contingent

social and cultural circumstances. From this viewpoint we can see how 'worlds' generate their own systems of causation. Systems of causation are based on experience (Douglas 1975: 276), and they vary as experiences differ. This is not to deny that certain objective causes produce certain objective effects in human society. Thus, a minor fall in the average temperature in Iceland during the so-called Little Ice Age (a climatic pessimum reached in late seventeenth century) may have produced years of farming failure in this marginal agricultural area. It is not self-evident or objectively true, however, that it should also have entailed starvation and misery. To 'explain' the course of Icelandic history we must analyse the total environment of Icelanders, including the *cultural* resources which prevented them from exploiting their arid environment 'appropriately'. Not only do worlds create their own systems of causation, based in culturally mediated experience, but such 'causal systems' in turn greatly influence the course of events.

This important point is illustrated also by Knudsen's analysis of the Corsican system of blood revenge, the so-called vendetta. Here compromised male honour was seen as a natural cause for killing, which in turn greatly affected local social structures by separating allies from enemies in a society which had no clear-cut kinship boundaries. Thus, identifying the object of the historicized social anthropology requires that people's own worlds be taken into account. Only then can we transcend the 'temporal causation' of the historians and discuss the why of particular developments from a truly anthropological perspective.

THE MAKING OF HISTORY

The registration of events in the synchronic dimension has its counterpart in the diachronic dimension. The recollection of events also follows the logic of social significance. Like the narrative of culture, the story of the past is therefore a selective account of the actual sequence of events, but it is no random selection.

Not all events survive in memory. As Anton Blok points out, the intersection of history and memory is central to any purportedly 'historical' anthropology. Memory is far from mechanical. For events to become part of 'history' they have to be or to have been experienced as significant. This point is not as self-evident as it may appear, because it is not only a question of obvious 'memorability'. It is an expression of a much more profound truth: the structuring of history, or the selective memory, is not solely imposed retrospectively (Ardener 1989). Although the universe created and memorized in history is relative to a series of successive presents, memorability is identified synchronically. This implies that contemporary event registration is always the baseline for the trace left in history by any present instant. Thus, while people always embed their present in the past by encompassing the existentially unique in the conceptually familiar (Sahlins 1985: 146), they also and at the same time inform their future 'history'. Our object of investigation is certainly a *synthesis* of diachrony and synchrony.

Relative memorability, then, is the trace left by previous (re)constructions of social space. Phrased differently, the retrospective recasting of events in the writing of history is a continuation of the contemporary process of event registration. Event-richness or event-poverty in the synchronic dimension and in contemporary experience is correlated with historical density in the diachronic perspective (Ardener 1989; Hastrup 1989).

This point has an important implication for our dealing with the past in that it reinstates social experience and the popular recollection of the past as vital elements in any writing of history. Traditionally, records were the only acceptable evidence of history, but from the anthropological perspective recollections are equally valid material for the reconstruction of the past not 'in spite of' but precisely 'because of' the significant cultural selection inherent in them. A recent concrete confirmation of this point is found in Rosaldo's (1980) work on Ilongot headhunting.

In some sense the sprouting 'oral history' is based in a corresponding acknowledgement of the validity of popular recollection (see, e.g., Vansina 1985). The perspective allows for a recognition of human beings as both subjects and objects of history. It is part of the current anthropological wisdom that there is a fundamental continuity between social space and the individuals who constitute it (Ardener 1987: 39). In other words, 'social forms can never shape human beings completely, because social forms owe their own shape to the fact that human beings are social agents with ideas of social forms' (Hollis 1985: 232). This is no less important when we are dealing with the making of history. No people is simply a victim of history, even though many peoples may have been victimized by particularly forceful notions of history (cf. e.g., Wolf 1982).

Because of the peculiar continuity between social space and its individuals, people are to a large extent authors of their own concepts in that they are responsible for their own actions (Sahlins 1985: 152). Although born at a particular moment of history and into a particular culture, people also take responsibility for whatever culture has made them. Even when powerlessness is part of social experience, as was the case with the Icelanders of some four 'dark' centuries (Hastrup 1990a), people remain the defining consciousness of social space. Culture may indeed recondition the conditions (Boon 1982: 114). This in fact provides the basis for the idea of exploding the Western concept of history by the anthropological concept of culture that is the aim of this work.

Until recently, the Enlightenment quest for what Whitehead called the 'One in Many' has dominated historical investigation and led us to believe that there was just one modern, linear, cumulative history that was distinctly European while the rest of the world was without history. *Other Histories* shows the opposite: there remain Many in the One.

REFERENCES

Ardener, Edwin (1982) 'Social anthropology, language, and reality', in David Parkin (ed.) *Semantic Anthropology*, ASA Monograph 22, London: Academic Press.
—— (1987) 'Remote areas: some theoretical considerations', in A. Jackson (ed.) *Anthropology at Home*, ASA Monograph 25, London: Tavistock.
—— (1989) 'The construction of history: "vestiges of creation" ', in E. Tonkin, M. McDonald, and M. Chapman (eds) *History and Ethnicity*, ASA Monograph 27, London: Routledge.
Beattie, John (1964) *Other Cultures*, London: Cohen and West.
Boon, James A. (1982) *Other Tribes, Other Scribes*, Cambridge: Cambridge University Press.
Braudel, Fernand (1980) *On History*, Chicago: University of Chicago Press.
Chapman, M., M. McDonald, and E. Tonkin (1989) 'Introduction: history and social anthropology', in E. Tonkin, M. McDonald, and M. Chapman (eds) *History and Ethnicity*, ASA Monograph 27, London: Routledge.
Douglas, Mary (1975) 'Self-evidence', in *Implicit Meanings: Essays in Anthropology by Mary Douglas*, London: Routledge and Kegan Paul.

Evans-Pritchard, E. E. (1964) *Social Anthropology and Other Essays*, New York: Free Press.

Fabian, Johannes (1983) *Time and the Other: How Anthropology Makes its Object*, New York: Columbia University Press.

Harbsmeier, Michael (1989) 'World histories before domestication', *Culture and History* 5: 93–132.

Hastrup, Kirsten (1985) *Culture and History in Medieval Iceland: An Anthropological Analysis of Structure and Change*, Oxford: Clarendon Press.

—— (1987a) 'Fieldwork among friends', in A. Jackson (ed.) *Anthropology at Home*, ASA Monograph 25, London: Tavistock.

—— (1987b) 'The reality of anthropology', *Ethnos* 52: 287–300.

—— (1989) 'The prophetic condition', in E. Ardener, *The Voice of Prophecy and Other Essays*, ed. M. Chapman, Oxford: Blackwell.

—— (1990a) *Nature and Policy in Iceland 1400–1800: An Anthropological Analysis of History and Mentality*, Oxford: Clarendon Press.

—— (1990b) *Island of Anthropology: Studies in Icelandic Past and Present*, Odense: Odense University Press.

Hodder, Ian (1982) *Symbols in Action: Ethnoarchaeological Studies of Material Culture*, Cambridge: Cambridge University Press.

Hollis, Martin (1985) 'Of masks and men', in M. Carrithers, S. Collins, and S. Lukes (eds) *The Category of the Person: Anthropology, Philosophy, History*, Cambridge: Cambridge University Press.

Jones, Gareth Stedman (1976) 'From historical sociology to theoretical history', *British Journal of Sociology* 27, 3.

Knudsen, Anne (1989) *En ø i Historien: Korsika, Historisk Antropologi 1730–1914*, Copenhagen: Basilisk.

Kuper, Adam (1988) *The Invention of Primitive Society*, London: Routledge.

Leach, Edmund (1989) 'Tribal ethnography: past, present, future', in E. Tonkin, M. McDonald, and M. Chapman (eds) *History and Ethnicity*, ASA Monograph 27, London: Routledge.

Lévi-Strauss, Claude (1966) *The Savage Mind*, London: Weidenfeld and Nicolson.

Lewis, I. M. (1968) *History and Social Anthropology*, ASA Monograph 7, London: Tavistock.

Löfgren, Orvar (1987) 'Colonizing the territory of historical anthropology', *Culture and History* 1: 7–30.

Lowenthal, David (1985) *The Past Is a Foreign Country*, Cambridge: Cambridge University Press.

Mair, Lucy (1969) *Anthropology and Social Change*, London School of Economics Monographs on Social Anthropology 38.

Maitland, F. W. (1936) [1899] *The Body Politic: Selected Essays*, ed. H. D. Hazeltine, G. Lapsley, and P. H. Winfield, Cambridge: Cambridge University Press.

Paine, Robert (1989) 'Israel: Jewish identity and competition over "tradition" ', in E. Tonkin, M. McDonald, and M. Chapman (eds) *History and Ethnicity*, ASA Monograph 27, London: Routledge.

Peel, J. D. Y. (1989) 'The cultural work of Yoruba ethnogenesis' in E.

Tonkin, M. McDonald, and M. Chapman (eds) *History and Ethnicity*, ASA Monograph 27, London: Routledge.

Rosaldo, Renato (1980) *Ilongot Headhunting 1883–1974: A Study in Society and History*, Stanford: Stanford University Press.

Rowlands, M. J. (1987) 'Europe in prehistory: a unique form of primitive capitalism?', *Culture and History* 1: 63–78.

Sahlins, Marshall D. (1976) *Culture and Practical Reason*, Chicago: University of Chicago Press.

—— (1981) *Historical Metaphors and Mythical Realities*, Ann Arbor: University of Michigan Press.

—— (1985) *Islands of History*, Chicago: University of Chicago Press.

Schechner, Richard (1981) 'Restoration of behavior', *Visual Communication* 7, 3: 2–45.

Shweder, Richard A. (1984) 'Preview: a colloquy of culture theorists', in R. A. Shweder and R. A. LeVine (eds) *Culture Theory: Essays on Mind, Self, and Emotion*, Cambridge: Cambridge University Press.

Vansina, Jan (1985) *Oral Tradition as History*, Madison: University of Wisconsin Press.

Wolf, Eric (1982) *Europe and the People without History*, Berkeley: University of California Press.

Chapter 1

History and the people without Europe

John Davis

My title acknowledges an intellectual debt to Eric Wolf, whose unique ability to put studies of other cultures into their proper context in political economy is indispensably inspiring. If I alter the order of the words it is to draw attention to other possibilities of history: What is thought about the past, like if the thinkers do not belong to a culture with the European tradition of historical inquiry? By this I mean to argue that if we wish to incorporate history into our analysis and explanation of social activity, we must pay some attention to the ways in which people construe the past. Thought about the past is a cultural activity which varies from place to place and from time to time, and it is a consequential activity: when people take decisions, one of the things they consider is the past.

Following Lisón Tolosana (1966), I have argued elsewhere that anthropologists should pay close attention to the social relations of the production of history (Davis 1989). The way knowledge is made affects knowledge itself – its shape and its content – and if knowledge in turn affects decisions, some part of our explanation of how social groups came to be as they are must be concerned with how people come to know the past. This chapter is concerned not so much with the social relations as with the raw materials of construing. The thought about the past which is produced in Europe is by and large dominated by a European set of concepts and notions. In general terms we expect our historians to produce a history in which chronological sequence is related to cause and effect and in which there is an unfolding story, and this seems to require mainly notions of linear time. These main elements – cause and effect, chronological sequence, linear time, a story – may not be present in quite the same mix in all thought about the past. For example, in Dresch's recent work on Yemen there is the following passage from a chronicle:

> The year 1262 (i.e., 1845, more or less).
> In the month of Rabi I a large star fell from west to east, bathing the earth in light stronger than the moon, beams of it being red and beams white. It crashed into the ground toward the east in about the time it takes to read the surah of Fidelity. As it went over there was a powerful noise like thunder. After this in those same months there were heavy rains and fearful strikes of lightning which destroyed many people. There were big hailstorms, each hailstone like an ostrich egg, which smashed houses and ripped through the roofs to destroy everyone inside except those whom God wished to spare.
> In the month of Rajab in this year one of the Sharifs of Mecca, whose name was Sayyid Ismail, set off toward Lower Yemen, always calling on people to support the jihad and to expel the Franks from Aden. A mass of people answered him. Then he arrived near Aden, about a farsakh away, and besieged the place until he was poisoned and died. Those warriors in God's cause who were in his company dispersed.
>   (al-Wasi'i 1928, cited in Dresch 1989: 174–5)

It is worth noting perhaps that the chronicle was written in the twentieth century: it is not an ancient document, although it is very similar in 'style and language' to the chronicles written some centuries before (Dresch 1989: 174). The problem here is that although there is meticulous chronology there is no essential plot (to use Dresch's word): what chronicles record is the exceptional and strange, whether natural or social, and we find it difficult to understand what it is that filters out the relevant from the irrelevant. The discussion in this chapter is concerned, then, with what history is like when concepts and notions are different from those which we have been led to expect from our experience of reading history. And if we can pinpoint differences, we might go on to speculate about the consequences of these differences. As I have said, I believe that thought about the past at least potentially can have consequences for present action.

This is not an argument for hermeneutics. I do not suggest that reality is in any simple sense a creation of human minds and social relations: things are as they are, and they came to be as they did. And they are in principle knowable, rather than simply interpretable. This is quite clear in the case of (say) major disasters: a volcano erupts, a population dies, and its interpretation of what has happened is largely beside the point. This is also true of many kinds of human action: for instance, in the twenty years after Italy's invasion of Libya in 1911 some 30–40 per cent of the population, mostly men, were killed or imprisoned or went into exile. The demographic consequences were real, whatever the interpretations Libyan or Italian survivors put on them: the decisions people took in those and subsequent years were inescapably in that context, since some options had been closed. Another instance: when a contemporary government decides to invest in nuclear power, resources are committed and are hence unavailable for anything else; within fairly broad limits, patterns of energy production and pricing are determined for a lifetime or so. And for a couple of millennia or so people will have to devote resources to protecting themselves from the waste: for thirty to sixty generations our descendants will be constrained to some extent by decisions taken by our scientists, politicians, and bureaucrats in the last thirty years. A purely interpretive account of history, maintaining that social order came to be so because people construed their history in one way or another, seems to miss the uninterpretably determining power of the past.

The reverse error is to take the past as a given; it is one that our predecessors were more liable to fall into than we are. When Evans-Pritchard remarked that we should not mistake the irreversible for the inevitable, he was, I think, warning against what might be called culminatory history. Anthropologists arrived in 'a society' or 'a community' and asked, among other things, 'How did this situation arise?' From records and books and reminiscences, they constructed a path which led from the past to the present and which purported to demonstrate how the present was a culmination of what had gone before. It is one of the virtues of Wolf's book, and of those of his friends John Cole and Jane and Peter Schneider, that their work is suffused with the sense that things might have turned out otherwise, could have been different, and that the irretrievable past is not inevitable (Cole and Wolf 1974; Schneider and Schneider 1976; Wolf 1982). On the contrary: without structure and without social relations, events are essentially arbitrary.

Therefore it seems to me that an entirely hermeneutic or interpretative account of history misses important points: we have to draw a line – and it may be a dotted or fuzzy one – between the determining power of past decisions and the room for manoeuvre which our common human propensity to interpret creates within those constraints. And when we consider the question of how a particular state of affairs came to be, we have to balance the explanatory weight of damned linearity, of one-thing-after-another, with the interpretative capacity of human populations.

KINDS OF THOUGHT ABOUT THE PAST

The field of 'thought about the past' is complex and is not confined to history. For academic purposes it is possible to distinguish four kinds which seem to be quite different in their structure and implications.

Autobiography and its vicarious off-shoot, biography, are concerned with the life and deeds of a person. We think of them as a universal activity, and I guess that they are: at any rate, let us assume that nearly all of us could give accounts of our lives so far, as well as of the main deeds and the character of one or two others. We have no problem, either, with the idea that the events and deeds which are taken to be important are of different kinds or with the idea that people will try to hide different kinds of shameful or humiliating events. What we do expect is that autobiography will be linear: people necessarily experience one thing after another, birth, marriage, and death following each other, usually in that order. Moreover, and attached to the notion of linearity, our lives are to some extent cumulative: after a while we become experienced at particular activities, and we may avoid others which we know we are not often successful at. My guess, again, is that this is universal: experienced magicians and gardeners in the Trobriands seem to share a generic quality of expertise and confidence with mechanics and water engineers in Libya, pruners and wine-makers in southern Italy, or indeed the experienced committee men of the University of Kent. This does not seem problematic, but it may be a rather too easy assumption, at any rate so far as linearity is concerned: Connerton's discussion of oral history suggests that linear autobiography is in fact fairly rare and is characteristic of the ruling groups in Western-style states:

> the writers of memoirs see their life as worth remembering because they are, in their own eyes, someone who has taken decisions which . . . changed part of their social world. . . . They have been inserted into the structure of dominant institutions and have been able to turn that structure to their own ends.
>
> (Connerton 1989: 19)

Underdogs, he suggests, do not insert their lives into the same 'narrative home' and use, rather, a cyclical framework for their accounts of themselves; so oral historians have found that their efforts to impose a chronological sequence on working-class lives disorient their informants and can distort their information. I am not at all sure that the only alternative to Leach's nautical almanac (Leach 1954; 1961) is cyclical time, as Connerton seems to think, but the suggestion that linear time is associated with statesmanship resonates with Herzfeld's (1987) accounts of Greek villages and with my own attempts to understand Qaddafi's manipulation of calendars in the Libyan revolution (Davis 1987: 58–69).

The second kind of thought about the past is one which abstracts events from their context in the past and presents them as precedents, examples of how things should or should not be done: incidents, events become examples of this or that rather than links in a chain of cause and effect. The evidence from without Europe is unequivocal. Dresch remarks of battles between Yemenis and Turks that

> even now, men will take one over the ground and point out in detail where the tribesmen stood, and where the Turks. But they rarely place events in a sequence. Indeed, it is usually impossible to co–ordinate different local accounts without the help of history books.
>
> (Dresch 1989: 223)

And these books were produced by quite different people, concerned with telling the story not of tribes against Turks but of the unfolding growth of the Yemeni state or the consolidation of the community of Muslims (Dresch 1989: 223). The history of the tribes was fragmented among the tribes, he says, and this

was congruent with the divisions between tribes and tribal sections: 'it is only the opposition (registered in spatial boundaries)
between tribes that gives most events their value'. Events were
remembered because they exemplified the oppositions and demonstrated the equivalence if not the equality of the segments.
The tenth-century poet and genealogist al-Hamdani recorded the
wars between Hashid and Bakil, Hamdan and Khawlan, Hamdan
and Murad, but he did not give any of them a date, and he did
not say who won and who lost (Dresch 1989: 178). It is linear
history which is the story of how one group comes to dominate
another, of how structures of dominance are created and
defended and strengthened. Precedental history is a series of
snapshots, a 'set of examples of the working of right principle'
(Davis 1987: 111), and does not record the creation of hierarchy.

These examples are from relatively stateless people or from
people who were subjects of states but who from time to time
and situation to situation acted and talked as if they were stateless. But of course it is not only those people who use precedental
accounts of the past: the judicial process of the Barotse, for
instance, was constituted from precedent, like the British
common law; and it could be argued that all reference to tradition is an appeal to precedent.

The third kind of thought about the past is myth; but we tend
to distance it from thought about the past by representing myths
as untrue accounts, and typically we write them in the present
tense. While Lévi-Strauss's Asdiwal is written in the present, his
source (in Boas's compilations) is in fact in the past tense. Tenses
are, I recognize, a difficult issue in some North American lan-
guages, but myths are generally presented: Leach retells Genesis
in the present tense, even though the original is emphatically in
the past and is taken by some people to be an accurate record
of events (Davis n.d.). The point here is that if myths are taken
to be more real than our customary use of language allows,
they may have consequences and hence explain some aspects of
people's decisions. In fact, in general terms, people do take
myths as records in some circumstances and as fanciful tales in
others. The Uduk of the Sudan-Ethiopian border, for instance,
distinguished stories from true words but not always in one con-
sistent way: the boundaries were flexible and permeable. James
found that it was difficult to get Uduk to recount a myth (James
1979: 60), and people who did mixed myth and 'true words'.

When she was collecting traditional tales from Bukko, who was an Uduk expert, she reports, 'we couldn't stop him switching from retailing myths to giving his opinions on present day affairs; nor could we stop him from inserting . . . his own extra anecdotes and historical snippets into "traditional" symbolic folklore' (p. 77). And she concludes: 'Myth and history are clearly "not the same thing". But nor is it possible to separate them, regarding history as what actually happened and myth as its fictional representation' (p. 85). In fact the language and imagery of 'true words' and 'stories' were intertwined, reflecting and informing each other. It is too easy for us to distance myth, to say that it is not really about the past – the real past which academic historians, for instance, try to uncover. But the association may in fact be very close, and some people, some of the time, may take it for real.

Finally, we have history – the Uduk's 'true words' about the past. The type of history is a chronological linear account of the unfolding of a story, suffused with notions of development from origins, of following the traces, even of uncovering processes. But the practices of historians are more complex than the type. Barthes's brilliant and amusing account of what historians do when they write history includes a survey of the games they play with time. Members of the *Annales* school, with their emphasis on mentalities and the historical ethnography of the common man, produce a kind of snapshot history, a series of precedents. But most history has a plot and is associated with the origin and development of the major institutions of state, church, industry. It is this kind of thought about the past which we anthropologists tend to use when we try to give an account of how Libyans or Yemenis or Uduk came to be as they were in the 1970s or 1980s.

These four kinds of thought about the past – autobiography, precedent, myth, history – are perhaps not the only kinds, but they are sufficient to maintain an argument that thought about the past is not a monopoly of historians or of people who are for the time being thinking history. Of course, it may be argued that history is the most interesting and valuable of the four because it has a greater tendency to reality; but that is not the point I am trying to attack or defend. Rather, if we allow that people interpret their experience and base current decisions in part on that knowledge, then we have to incorporate those modes of thought into our accounts of how societies came to be as they are. I want to suggest now that one of the more important components of thought about the past is notions of time, and these again are not constants, givens, the same the world over. Local times are ways of representing duration, irreversibility of change, and recurrence, and they vary at least in the emphasis that they place on these three different experiences.

What I mean may be clearer from a particular case, and it seems sensible to take identity, for which time – the past, history, myth, precedent, and biography – is absolutely central. Philosophers who discuss personal identity nowadays seem to have relatively little difficulty in accepting that at any given moment you and I are indeed different people. What is difficult is to show how one can be the same person one was, say, five years ago. The issues are essentially to do with time and memory, and philosophers have always discussed them with reference to linear-time autobiographies (Reid 1975 [1785]: 114).[1] I note, in passing, that these are one subset of the *genre* and are perhaps associated with state's men. The same issues clearly arise, however, in relation to collective identities: there is no identity – ethnic or other group of any kind – without a past. If you were employed as a consultant applied anthropologist to construct a collective identity, the first thing you would do would be to draw the boundaries of the collectivity, and then you would create customs, traditions – a history, all tending to show that the collectivity is old and encrusted with the signs of antiquity and hence has a claim to recognition by significant others, in this case, usually governments of nation-states.

IDENTITY AND THE PAST

The Uduk seem to have used what Leach (1961) called a pendulum view of time,[2] which he thought was perhaps the most ancient and primitive one: on the fringes of the Ethiopian and Nile civilizations, they were subjected to periodic and recurrent devastation by slave raiders and livestock rustlers, by Nuer and Galla, and most recently by the parties to civil wars: they were periodically reduced to near-extinction. They then rebuilt, creating villages which were clusters of men around a core of surviving women; they achieved some prosperity and in due course were again laid waste. They alternated between life as matrilineal cultivating villagers and life as refugees, which they

represented to themselves as a reversion to the primordial mythical condition of being like dogs or antelopes in the bush – their
history thus a series of alternations between 'true words' and
myth, each used to illustrate the other. A man who recounts
myths slips easily into contemporary history; a person who tells
of his own life, of his grandfather's life, uses myth as a graphic
shorthand for conditions in time of disaster: personal and collective memory are intertwined with traditional symbolic stories.

'The present-day world of the Uduk', says James (1979: 234),
'can be received (by us) on its own terms, as yet another exotic
way of life and thought'. It is tempting to imagine that we are
the ones with fluid boundaries and uncertainty, while matrilineal
cultivators are culturally self-sufficient and sure of themselves.
The theme of James's work, however, is that Uduk are marginal,
interstitial: they are those who survived, a composite of an 'ethnographic remnant' (James 1979: 4) and strangers who have
settled with them. No Uduk in fact call themselves Uduk;[3] the
northerners, for instance, refer to themselves as the people of
'the homeland', and that word is itself borrowed from the language of a Nilotic people (James 1979: 234). Uduk-speakers
generally are bi- or multilingual, showing interest and facility in
other tongues. Uduk thought about the past contains a series of
alternations between civilization and peace, on the one hand,
and attacks, enslavement, and reversion to the life of antelopes
and dogs, on the other:[4]

> they are, and know themselves to be, both freed slaves in the
> literal sense, in part, and also a people spared by God from
> the very real possibility of historical extinction. Their society
> in the past has been built up in the face of insecurity, and the
> people of the homeland are those who have struggled to clear
> the woodland and settle down together.
>
> (James 1979: 16)

To these people are added waifs and strays from the bush:
'bringing in wild and lost people and making them into a part
of the moral community of the homeland is basic to the people's
understanding of who they are and how their society has come
to be what it is' (James 1979: 16). Furthermore, the central social
ritual of the northern Uduk (the Gurunya) was a protective
one, performed when people thought that newborn children were
unlikely to live. The ritual turned the endangered children into

strays, dogs or birds, who were then supported and cared for by the whole community in an elaborate collective effort to secure (in James's striking phrase) the survival of the weakest and hence of the people of the homeland.

Uduk had a language; they knew who was a person of the homeland and who was not, although they were not exclusive about that. Their rituals were drawn from various sources, and the name they used for themselves was from a foreign language. Their knowledge of the past was a combination of biography, myth, and shared memory of survival as individuals. They knew themselves to be a remnant and spoke of this 'sometimes with frank acceptance, sometimes with resentful passion, and sometimes with humour' (James 1979: 18). For present purposes the force of James's analysis lies in the way in which this culturally and socially eclectic group maintained groupishness without maintaining boundaries of membership. The point is that although Uduk knew very well who they were and who was not Uduk, they had no identity of the kind we encounter in Europe: they did not construe themselves as a self-conscious cultural or ethnic group with a history and traditions which constituted an entitlement. If I can try to put this more positively, it might be possible to say, very tentatively, that their mythical origins were part of an alternating series of oppositions rather than part of a series of causes and effects such as explain (say) the distinctiveness of Ukrainians in contemporary Britain. Their main and significant boundary was the mythico-historical one between being people and being antelopes or dogs. The dog's life was ever present, in fact and in myth, and those who were Uduk were those who had survived the swings of the pendulum.

The Yemeni scene is characteristically more complex altogether. It seems to me that we have to take account of three kinds of identity, all of which were available to Yemeni tribesmen although perhaps other Yemenis had a more restricted range. The three are associated with kinds of thought about the past and with kinds of notion about time. Tribesmen knew themselves to be members of a tribe: they had a territory and a descent, and they were 'always in a space whose value derives from its position among others like it', so that what one did there took its meaning in large part from where one was when one did it (Dresch 1989: 75). Tribes had always been where they were, and tribesmen came from one 'grandfather': they were brothers, and that was the source of their cohesion and opposition. Identity in this case was oppositional; it denoted opposition to other tribes deemed to be equivalent and equal. The basis was genealogy, and genealogies are the nearest thing to a generative model that anthropologists encounter: they propose a proper sequence of events (essentially one of begetting), but have no necessary location in time: the genealogies of tribes were therefore the ideal framework for setting out a snapshot, precedental, past. Individual and family identity was in some ways dissociated from tribal identity. One could be a good man from a good family, or from not so strong a line, and so on. But whereas Yemeni tribes and their third or fifth or ninth parts were fixed and had always been where they were, individual families were and knew themselves to be really quite mobile: the character of incomer (*naqa'il*) was relatively commonplace, and indeed men did not use a tribal genealogy to describe their personal descent: 'men or sections who are known to have joined the tribe are as much "from one forebear" as those who have shared the tribe's eponym for as long as anyone knows' (Dresch 1989: 78). Although all men claimed descent from the remotest ancestors, Dresch says, scarcely anyone knew any personal forebears more remote than a great-grandfather. It is relatively easy for us as outsiders to assimilate family and tribe, because they seem to share genealogy and the idiom of honour. But the honour of families does not overlap entirely with the honour of tribes, and the three-generation biography-based family past does establish dominance and inequality within the tribes.[5] Families can go up and down, while tribes remain theoretically fixed.[6] The point of this is that individual identity, derived from biographical and autobiographical time, was reckoned differently from collective identity (precedental time). And the structure of history and the kinds of events recorded were different in the two cases: the 'always so' of the tribal past – fragmented, unplotted, non-culminatory – was illustrated with a series of vignettes of correct, honourable behaviour, and the past was segmented and timeless.

All this contrasts with the learned tradition concerned with the unity of the Muslim community and with the deeds of the imams, in which tribes were a residue and tribal identities 'peripheral' (Dresch 1989: 179). In effect, when tribesmen were good Muslims and respectful subjects they were ignored in the learned history, and when they were not they were treated as pagan, uncivilized, and reprehensible. In the histories of the seven-teenth-century wars against the Turks, for example, the tribes are a kind of human territory, a terrain which the armies pass across, even though the tribesmen fought in the wars and in one role or another were the main force at the imams' disposal. In the contemporary world, 'Yemeni' is an identity available to tribesmen, and it is the culmination of the history of the Yemeni state. The point is, I think, that this history (and the identity which it supports) is 'constructed explicitly in time and so is capable of forming a single story' as tribal thought and talk about the past is not. The one is hierarchical and chronological, the other fragmented, segmentary, and egalitarian: they do not mesh, and do not conflict, because they have no common ground: tribal identities, like tribal histories, are not summable into those of larger groups.

THE CONSEQUENCES OF THE PAST

'Thought about the past' is an important element in social creativity because it is part of the information which people use in making decisions which affect the future. What I have tried to illustrate is that history (linear, plotted) is not the only way in which people know the past: in particular, people do not produce developmental or culminatory accounts of the past when they use one or another non-linear notion of time.

Notions of time are only one of the factors of production: I believe very firmly that events are themselves a major raw material, and in some respects they are not convertible by inter-pretation. And in addition to these raw materials one has to take into account, as Lisón Tolosana did, the social relations among producers of history. The issues, then, are complex and ramified, and I do not claim to have given a comprehensive or synoptic account of history here. What I have argued is that there is an association between kinds of identity and kinds of notion of time. I have contrasted in a very schematic way the oppositional groupishness of Yemeni tribesmen and the inclusive and eclectic self-image of Uduk villagers – both of them, I think, very differ-ent from the ethnic identities with which we are familiar in our own social worlds. Those are typically linear, tending to show that Catalan or Breton or Jewish identities are ancient and (having a place in history) therefore have a claim to political representation in a nation-state. The issue of identity is particularly apt because it is crucially established with reference to the past: the question is, however, what past, and I have tried to show that pasts are not all construed in the same way.

We European anthropologists have a tendency to think of history as an account of 'what really happened' and to approach rather gingerly those other accounts of the past which could never have happened (as the Uduk never were antelopes) or which did not really happen quite as tribesmen in Libya or Yemen say they did. What I want to suggest, in practical terms, is that our kind of account of the past is only part of an explanatory history. We too are entitled to our cultural exercises, and doing our kind of history is undoubtedly useful and interesting. But if we want to explain the power of the past in shaping contemporary exotic societies we should bear in mind that the actors in that history may have been taking a different but coherent view of the past.

NOTES

1 The locus classicus is Thomas Reid's criticism of Locke's memory theory of personal identity:

> Suppose a brave officer to have been flogged when a boy at school for robbing an orchard, to have taken a standard from the enemy in his first campaign, and to have been made a general in advanced life; suppose, also, which must be admitted to be possible, that, when he took the standard he was conscious of his having been flogged at school, and that, when made a general, he was conscious of his having taken the standard, but had absolutely lost the consciousness of his flogging.
>
> These things being supposed, it follows from Mr Locke's doctrine, that he who was flogged at school is the same person who took the standard, and that he who took the standard is the same person who was made a general. Whence it follows . . . that the general is the same person with him who was flogged at school. But the general's consciousness does not reach so far back as his flogging; therefore, according to Mr Locke's doctrine, he is not the same person who was flogged. Therefore the general is, and at the same time is not, the same person with him who was flogged at school.
>
> (Reid 1975 [1785]: 116)

2 The 'discontinuity of repeated contrasts', Leach suggests, is 'probably the most elementary and primitive of all ways of regarding time' (1961: 134), and he takes the pendulum and the tick-tock of clocks

as types of this representation. Cyclical time, he suggests, is a product of religious thought, a reassurance that 'Time Itself' repeats itself and does not come to an end (p. 130). Tick-tock is interestingly emblematic of the complexity of our contemporary representations of time, since (obviously) the clock (which goes 'tick-tock') postdates the elementary form of the representation of time. Moreover, clocks themselves convert the pendulum swing of 'discontinuity of repeated contrasts' to the progressive and repetitive cycles of analogue chronometers. In fact, even pendulum or spring-driven clocks do not make two contrasted sounds: using an oscilloscope, for instance, reveals a much more complex pattern of noise. And you can conduct the following experiment as you lie in bed with an old-fashioned alarm clock beside you: follow the sounds by saying with the clock, 'tick; tock; tick; tock'. And then change step: 'tick; tock; tick; tick; tock tick; tock'. Even though you may be convinced that clocks make two distinct sounds, and can hear them, you can represent both sounds with either word. The alternating oppositions of hickory dickory dock are a cultural artefact bearing no mechanical relation whatever to the noise of clockworks. I conclude from this that we jumble the really quite sophisticated representations of the analogue clock with the most elementary representation of alternating opposites.

3 That word may be from the Arabic *atiqa* – a freed slave or one whose life has been spared by God.

4 In their stories about life before civilization much emphasis is placed on the fact that they spoke like dogs, did not have proper language, and, for instance, did not know the word for 'mother's brother'.

5 The link between individual and collective identity is formed by the concepts of honour [*sharaf*, *'ird/'ard*, *naqa'*, *'ayb*, *wajh*] which largely overlap: 'the one term in this set which is used of individuals but not of tribes is *wajh* ("face" . . .)' (p. 79).

6 Dresch's ethnography describes and analyses the ways in which this theoretical balance was never an actuality.

REFERENCES

Cole, John W., and Wolf, Eric R. (1974) *The Hidden Frontier: Ecology and Ethnicity in an Alpine Valley*, London: Academic Press.

Connerton, Paul (1989) *How Societies Remember*, Cambridge: Cambridge University Press.

Davis, John (1987) *Libyan Politics: Tribe and Revolution, the Zuwaya and Their Government*, London: I. B. Tauris.

—— (1989) 'The social relations of the production of history', in E. Tonkin, M. McDonald, and M. Chapman (eds) *History and Ethnicity*, ASA Monograph 27, London: Routledge.

—— (n.d.) 'Tense in ethnography: some practical considerations', in Judith Okely (ed.) *Autobiography and Anthropology*, London: Routledge, in press.

Dresch, Paul (1989) *Tribes, Government, and History in Yemen*, Oxford: Clarendon Press.

Herzfeld, Michael (1987) *Anthropology through the Looking-Glass: Critical Ethnography in the Margins of Europe*, Cambridge: Cambridge University Press.

James, Wendy R. (1979) *Kwanim Pa, the Making of the Uduk People: An Ethnographic Study of Survival in the Sudan-Ethiopian Borderlands*, Oxford: Clarendon Press.

Leach, Edmund R. (1954) 'Primitive time-reckoning', in C. Singer, E. J. Holmyard, and A. R. Hall (eds) *A History of Technology*, vol. 1, *From the Earliest Times to the Fall of the Ancient Empires*, Oxford: Clarendon Press.

—— (1961) 'Two essays concerning the symbolic representation of time', in *Rethinking Anthropology*, London School of Economics Monographs in Social Anthropology 22.

Lisón Tolosana, Carmelo (1966) *Belmonte de los Caballeros: A Sociological Study of a Spanish Town*, Oxford: Clarendon Press.

Reid, Thomas (1975) [1785] 'Of Mr Locke's account of our personal identity', in John Perry (ed.) *Personal Identity*, Berkeley: University of California Press.

Schneider, Jane, and Schneider, Peter (1976) *Culture and Political Economy in Western Sicily*, New York: Academic Press.

Wolf, Eric R. (1982) *Europe and the People without History*, Berkeley: University of California Press.

Chapter 2

Making history in southern Italy

Thomas Hauschild

The anthropologist, psycho-analyst, and cosmopolite Georges Devereux (1983; see also 1950) once tried to outline the dilemma of human existence *in extremis*. In a remarkable essay on apocalyptic thinking published shortly before his death, he argued that the destruction of the world is always as much a delusion as it is a reality. Thus we will rarely be sure whether we are dealing with actual dangers or – as was so often the case – chimerae of the apocalypse which mankind seems to have feared since the beginning of time. Devereux sees human beings as perpetually trapped in self-delusion. It is only when individual or collective apocalypses (de Martino 1977) present themselves that we will have the answer.

I would like to draw attention to a topic that is complementary to Devereux's apocalyptic theme. I spent two years in southern Italy (Hauschild 1985, 1986, 1987, 1990) in an effort to examine the way in which individuals and groups seek consolation in the face of life's risks by turning to the saints: talking to them, dreaming of them, presenting them with gifts, and celebrating them. Since historical themes play an important role in Christian discourse on the conquest of evil through the saints, I believe that by describing the results of my fieldwork I can also make a contribution to this book on anthropology and history.

THE FIRST WINTER: CONTRADICTIONS OF FIELDWORK

From the beginning, my fieldwork in Ripacandida, a mountain agrotown in southern Italy's Basilicata/Lucania region, was characterized by a series of contradictions – contradictions in my perception of what I was witnessing and in the information pro-

vided by my informants as well as contradictions between the
two. It is from these contradictions that the themes of this chapter evolved.

I had come to Italy to investigate what I had imagined to be
ancient religious concepts, and in doing so I was able to refer
to famous precursors such as George Dumas, Ernesto de Martino, Carlo Levi, and Pierpaolo Pasolini.[1] At the same time, the
first generation of British anthropologists of the Mediterranean
– Pitt-Rivers (1954), Kenny (1960), Boissevain (1966)[2] – had
taught me a harmonizing, functionalist and ahistorical approach
to popular belief. The people I talked to in Ripacandida
reinforced my opinion that I was concerned here with an immutable *festa antichissima* (age-old feast), but the long winter eve-
nings gave me a chance to observe that, precisely in the year of
my arrival, a festival committee consisting of young technocrats
had taken over the organization of the feast of the patron saint
and was trying to give it a modern touch by highlighting its
folkloristic and touristic aspects. Supposedly age-old customs
were being falsified, remodelled, and polished up before my
eyes.[3]

There was yet another contradiction: I had arrived in Ripacandida in the fall of 1982, and therefore I had not yet seen the
town's great feast in honor of its patron, St. Donatus, which is
celebrated in August. For a long time, I was confined to examining this event in the testimony of the townspeople about its latest
celebration. What caught my attention was that, on the one
hand, Ripacandidesi would emphasize how ridiculously low participation on the part of locals and pilgrims from the surrounding
villages was nowadays,[4] while, on the other, they were describing
a feast the dimensions of which exceeded my imagination: 15,000
pilgrims reportedly journey to this remote mountain town, and
donations are supposed to surpass many a major item in the
community's budget. My confusion in light of these contradictions peaked when I was invited to become a member of the
festival committee as a supposed specialist on religious traditions
and to join in shaping the tradition I was about to investigate.
As a member of the festival committee, I was given a vivid
impression of how 'tradition' is invented while having the oppor-
tunity to experience how the population resisted such attempts
at manipulation.[5]

This study of how people deal with the past has taught me to distinguish discourse from social and historical reality. It took some time before I was able to differentiate among the cyclical reality of the customs surrounding the St. Donatus cult, their transformation in time, people's reaction to this change, and the influence of nostalgic rhetoric about the past on ritual and political realities. Caught between these four poles of perception, I had to conduct my fieldwork on uncertain terrain between delusion and reality.

THE FIRST SUMMER: LEGENDS, CRISES, AND CYCLES

A central part of the Christian cult – including the cult of saints – is the reading and illustration of Christian texts, particularly legends.[6] It is on the basis of these texts that a particular saint is credited with competency in very specific worldly matters. This also manifests itself in the attributes of the statues of these saints: St. Michael, with the defeated dragon, is said to ward off evil in one's hour of death, while St. Anthony, engulfed in flames, is thought to guard against painful situations of shame as well as skin diseases.

As a metaphorical expression of the great Christian discourse on virtue and resurrection, the legend was taken up by the peasants of southern Italy – as by lay Catholics throughout the world – and moved a step farther towards concretization. The sacred past was set in relation to the most profane present. The saints acted in place of their earthly charges; their conquest of evil, the example they set, served to guarantee that the living would overcome the evil in the world. In this sense the legend drew worldly evil out of its historical context and placed it in a context of healing and redemption (de Martino 1958). Numerous ritual practices, such as the ones I was finally able to observe once summer had come, also fit into this timeless frame. Year after year, life in this small town is geared towards St. Donatus's cyclical return. Over and over again his arrival is met with enthusiasm – a circumstance that eclipses any theory of the inevitable bureaucratization of charisma (see Weber 1920: 203–4 and, on the following debate on secularization and revival, Berger 1967 and Greeley 1972).

At the same time, individuals will succeed in introducing their own personal crises into this great cycle (Van Gennep 1943: 95ff.; see also Belmont 1979: 40ff. on Van Gennep's 'biological' approach and his concepts of 'rhythms' of life and research). The feast of St. Donatus attracts people from all over Lucania who hope to be cured of epilepsy and other nervous disorders. The legendary martyred bishop was supposedly beheaded in Arezzo in the year 362 and is therefore often regarded in southern Italy as the saint of all 'afflictions that come from the head'. The despair of the afflicted and their relatives is transformed into prayers regularly directed at the saint and into cyclical visits to his shrine in Ripacandida. Participation in the procession dressed in the costume of the saint on three successive occasions during early childhood is part of the lives of many healthy people, who are thus prophylactically placed in the healing and redeeming context of identification with the saint for the rest of their lives. Whether because of cyclically staged tradition or acute personal crisis, the cult of the saint opens up this context through the mechanism of repetition compulsion and by virtue of the regularity and seemingly endless continuation of the cult's practices.

When young people, especially young men, temporarily display a reluctance to accept these practices, this does not necessarily worry their elders. They are accustomed to the observation that, as one of my informants put it, 'devotion increases with experience'. But this kind of utterance is part of a conversational strategy that makes it possible to integrate wholly uncyclical and novel phenomena into the cult's timeless context. At this point it suffices to note once more that the observation of the festival and statements such as the one just cited long led me to assume that the feast of St. Donatus was a survival of mediaeval – if not ancient – Christian culture. Historical evidence of age-old customs such as that of dressing up children in the costume of a saint (Lützenkirchen 1981: 46ff.) nourished my assumptions based on the information provided by my informants that this custom had indeed maintained a cyclical, imitative character for centuries.

THE SECOND WINTER: HISTORICAL CHANGE

Participation in the summer festival cycles was followed by another Lucanian winter, during which I set about examining the historical background of the events I had observed. My work in the archives and my conversations with Ripacandidesi about their past soon cast doubt on the image of a cyclical, immutable cult.

Among other things, both Ripacandidesi and pilgrims would regularly fasten bank-notes to the effigy of their saint using safety pins. One reason for observing this custom seemed to be the publicity it provided: the donor, the sum, and the recipient were visible to all. Nevertheless, I was surprised by the vehemence with which people defended it against the Church's attempts to modernize it. As late as 1981, riot police were forced to intervene when the bishop of Melfi tried to repress this custom as a pagan practice of bargaining with the saint allegedly carried over from antiquity. On this occasion an infuriated elderly woman went up and slapped His Eminence in the face. In contrast to this, another custom went almost unnoticed. During the modernization of the shrine in 1982, remnants of a St. Donatus scale which had been used for centuries to weigh the grain presented to the saint were taken away. As the ancient scale was being removed, a few pilgrims expressed their relief: 'Now that we can finally donate money, there's no need for us to transport those heavy sacks'. My research in the archives led to the discovery that the custom which was now so stubbornly defended had not emerged until about 1910, when a money economy gained ground. The more recent custom, tied to a money economy, was now being described as 'age-old' by opponents and advocates alike. In the meantime, the truly ancient custom based on barter and generalized reciprocity had faded into obscurity.

Similar confusion arose as I investigated the custom of having small and sick children and youths join the procession dressed up as the martyr bishop. Customs of this kind can be traced back to the beginnings of the Middle Ages (Lützenkirchen 1981; Kantorowicz 1965) and are regarded as characteristic of Italian cults of St. Donatus. Their goal is obvious: by imitating him in appearance, the young ones are to be familiarized with the concept of martyrdom, the saint's example being clearly impressed upon their minds. Not until I had engaged in lengthy conversations about the history of the feast did I realize, however, that although the custom was embedded in the history and nature of Catholicism, it had emerged in Ripacandida no earlier than in the fifties of this century. Until then, children had been dressed up as monks, modelled, for instance, on St. Anthony of Padua or the little Franciscan monk who accompanies the statue of St.

Donatus as an attribute. Not until the fifties, 'when all the money from the emigrants came', did people begin to dress children up as the bishop himself. Now families spare no expense in trying to outdo each other in presenting magnificent little bishops. The transformation of this seemingly archaic custom corresponded to the advancement of the Italian peasant to the status of an emigrant and later a landowner or pensioner. The general trend was away from the humble little monk to the bishop in all his splendour. The history of this seemingly unalterable and archaic custom clearly reflects the transition to a money economy and the proud self-portrayal of a new petite bourgeoisie.

Oddly enough, the history of these customs was very difficult to reconstruct. I had to resort to analysing old photographs, the correspondence of priests, and the testimony of a woman who, as a tailor, had introduced the new costume of St. Donatus in Ripacandida. Although my informants enjoyed speaking about the past, very often at great length, they had either forgotten about these changes or declined to bring up the subject themselves. For them, the essence of these practices had remained unchanged. Whether people dressed up as monk or bishop or whether they donated grain or money was of no greater importance. Perhaps a more intense confrontation with the changes that had taken place would have only disturbed their vision of an immutable cult of saint and community.[7]

THE SECOND SUMMER: IMAGINATION AND REALITY

Apart from the traditionalism of the Ripacandidesi there is, however, another reason for the difficulties I encountered in investigating change: the local priest actively obstructed my research efforts. Among other things, he declined to let me see the archives of a once powerful brotherhood in Ripacandida and tried to keep older townspeople from answering my questions. As far as my inquiry into the custom of pinning money onto effigies was concerned, I was later able to understand his reaction. Since the nineteenth century and probably even much earlier, the Ripacandidesi have been quarrelling with their priests over to whom the valuables presented to the saint actually belonged. In several tediously negotiated concordats it was laid down that donations made to the saint directly, for instance, by pinning money to his effigy, belonged to the civil festival committee. Thus the stubbornness with which the Ripacandidesi defended this custom had something to do with the defence of their rights as laymen against any infringement on the part of the clergy. Contrary to what the priest would have them believe, contagious magic and pagan *do ut des*[8] was not involved.

A related observation can be made about the brotherhoods. The priest had tried to bar my way to their archives and their legacy, which was preserved in the memory of witnesses of the time. Even in the late fifties, there had been a 'red brotherhood' in Ripacandida which endeavored to combine Catholicism and communism.[9] The twenties had seen intense conflicts over 'funerals without priests', 'processions infiltrated by communists', and fascist priests. The present priest, a Christian Democrat, wanted to obliterate all memory of these events and manipulate the symbolic wealth of the collective memory of the town's cultic past to his own ends. He was a 'conservative' in a double, highly ambiguous sense, and my research did not fit into his plans. To this day, he has the habit of deliberately ignoring me *in piazza* when I show up for a visit in Ripacandida.

The population countered the priest's manipulation of the past in a straightforward manner – by producing new legends. Thus even young people often claimed that the statue itself would provide an indication of whether or not the saint was pleased with the feast. If a festival was 'good', its cheeks would redden and its face radiate; if it was 'bad', its face would take on a sombre expression. A festival was 'good' when it did justice to the desire of laymen for the generous worldly program which customarily accompanies such feasts, when many costumed children joined in, and when plenty of money was pinned to the statue. It was 'bad' when controversies over these matters surfaced; this was an unmistakable warning to both the priest and the festival committee, and it was made on behalf of the saint. Fabricated reminiscences of past festivals during which the priest had had to take a back seat served as examples of 'good' feasts. I myself was regarded as an authority on 'good' festivals because, in the minds of the Ripacandidesi, I had now become a specialist and a defender of tradition. I was, however, not accorded the freedom of expression that the saint obviously had. 'Thomas, do you like the festival?' Over and over again, I had to answer yes.

Having been proclaimed a 'specialist', I became not only the object of rivalry over the collective past but also the personal witness of each and every one of my informants. Towards the end of my stay, the older people, in particular, had come to appreciate me as a confidant and an intermediary in the camp of the young. On countless occasions I was the target if not the victim of their nostalgic rhetoric: in the days of the forefathers, in *their* days, the feasts were much more beautiful and much bigger, the songs of the pilgrims more intense, the penitential rites more rigorous, the processions more arduous. This I certainly could not deny on the basis of my research. Of course, the transition from a system of barter to a money economy had altered the practice of making donations, and certainly the collective pilgrimage on foot had given way to a journey to the shrine in the family car. But still, year after year, people crowded around the statue by the thousands, excited and deeply moved. News of recent miracles circulated, and, as if it were a matter of course, the emigrant community of Ripacandidesi in Chicago still gathered around the saint (Rizzs 1981).[10] When seen in this light, the nostalgic, wistful rhetoric in reminiscence of past glory can also be seen as a clever way of making the saint the talk of the town again – of lending him a new voice.[11] I have collected dozens of legends in which the saint appears in a modern setting. He is seen wearing street clothes; he appears to people on the train and urges them to go to Ripacandida; he warns a reckless motorcyclist by briefly suspending his motorcycle in the air while still in motion; he intervenes during brain surgeries and shows up in intensive-care units. Doctors have their own children wear his costume because they, too, are afraid of epilepsy.

Another aspect that caught my attention was that the most nostalgic of all were often very successful in reviving the cult of St. Donatus in their own families. Grandchildren, preferably the offspring of their own children who had emigrated, were talked into wearing the costume under the pretext of the grandparents' incorrigible nostalgia. Thus they were again set on the path to imitation of the saint – which is certainly an unforgettable experience for a boy destined to become a computer specialist in Milan or New York. I myself saw how a sixteen-year-old girl from Milan who suffered from a mild psychic disorder was redirected by her grandmother from modern 'community psychiatry' to the community life of the devotees of St. Donatus and cured in the process. I also witnessed emigrants, successful businessmen in the prime of life, bursting into tears when they caught sight of the statue of the saint for the first time in twenty years. Here, family dynamics of transference and countertransference became a vehicle for the re-creation and rehabilitation of the past in the present and for the construction of an individual life history.[12]

Oral tradition seems to be subject to negotiation as a vehicle and a means of power serving individual as well as group interests (see Vansina 1965: 164ff. and, for recent discussion, Schramm 1988: 223ff.; Boelscher 1988: 28ff.; Dupré 1985). It manifests itself in talk about the past and thus contributes to shaping the future. Memories and original texts are adapted and varied: parts of the traditional text are left out and forgotten. There are occasional attempts to stamp out certain memories. Some parts of the traditional text are transformed and mythologized, while others are consciously defended and remembered almost too precisely.[13]

Thus memory becomes evocation and recounting becomes invocation, and in this discursive practice the individual finds his or her place, his or her vocation as a devotee of the saint. A certain continuity will remain in these creative adaptations as long as individually and politically motivated variations continue to revolve around that one centre: the saint, his statue, his legend, and the context of the Christian doctrine of salvation and church politics, which forms a dome over all.

REALITY, DISCOURSE, AND THE DIVINE

Whenever I try to depart from a scientific style and to approach the religious rhetoric of the Ripacandidesi, I realize that during my fieldwork different gods, that is to say, different modalities of meaning, collided.[14] At the beginning, I had run into considerable difficulties because I was unable to cope with the contradictions in the statements and the behaviour of my informants – to resolve the tension between discourse and reality. My functionalist and romantic myth of the everlasting faith of this supposed 'little community' blended with the romantic self-portrayal of the people of southern Italy. Under the influence of a powerful tradition of southern Italian studies, I had wanted to isolate the eternal magic of the 'real society' from the historical tradition of the 'official society'.[15] Then again, my materialism tended to prevent me from becoming fully aware of the continuity in historical change.[16] I seldom succeeded in finding words for the creative way in which the Ripacandidesi dealt with their past. They imitated the past while at the same time rewriting their history. They nostalgically lamented the decline of the old world while simultaneously renewing it.

Their god was not my god – not my functionalist, scientific god and least of all the abstract Protestant god of my youth. Their god was both concrete and abstract. 'What do you think of the concept of the Trinity?', I asked, whereupon Angelo Rondinella answered, 'The Trinity you can visit; it's in Venosa.' And only ten kilometres away, in Venosa's Trinitarian monastery, I found a strange group of statues: an old man with a white beard, a young man, and between them a white bird and a huge globe on which only three cities were indicated on the clearly outlined continents: Rome, New York, and Venosa.

'Do you want to hear about a dream I had?', Rosa Fortuna asked me. 'Go ahead', I said. She told me that she had dreamt of Jesus Christ. He appeared to her in dual form: in the shape of the crucified Lord, who suffered before her eyes, and in the shape of a little old man (which corresponded with a Lucanian narrative tradition of the 'old' Christ). The old man said, 'If you don't look at him, he must die.' Through devotion, the act of contemplating, the suffering and aging god is reborn. This corresponds to Kenneth Burke's (1970) theory of language and religion. The discourse analyst sees every language as something distinct from the things it describes – as having a life of its own. In this sense, all human mental activity creates something supernatural which must always be corrected in the natural world. Ripacandidesi know this; they know how valuable memory, language, and tradition are to political and psychic processes. They understand that language is something supernatural and that our talk paves the way for manifestation. In other words, they understand how language can sometimes be made efficacious.

Thus fieldworkers become witnesses and apostles and southern Italian peasants become language theorists. Seventy-year-old Carmela Quartariegg', one of my dearest friends in Ripacandida, gave me a piece of advice to take with me. As I understand it now, she drew my attention to the wavering nature of man, which does not seem to allow any scientific classification of closed belief systems. The greatest sign of affection is the warning of a friend – namely, the informant – about his own unreliability. At the same time, she warned me against being overly hasty and pointed out that discourse and reality must ultimately be reconciled, whether they are compatible or not. In short, she tried to provide me with instructions for the use of Devereux's world of perpetual self-delusion. She said:

> First, trust no one – least of all your friends. Friends can become traitors. Secondly, as the forefathers would say: 'Whoever departs from ancient paths knows what he is about to lose, but he does not know what he will find'. Thirdly, tradition is truth.

NOTES

1 Recent Anglo-American discourse on the historicity of anthropological approaches (Clifford and Marcus 1986) has yet to discover its Italian forerunner, Ernesto de Martino, who organized his writings on southern Italian culture in three layers: (1) the deconstruction of concepts of a romantic and pagan South, (2) the historical dimension of the phenomena studied in the field, and (3) the field data themselves and their socioeconomic context (see de Martino 1948; 1959: pt. 2, chaps. 6 and 7; Bronzini 1982; Gallini 1988; 1989). For a recent deconstruction of older traditions of projecting romantic attitudes on southern Italy, see Richter (1985); for a more general concept of exoticism as repetition of pre-existing 'images', see Kramer (1977; 1989).

2 Herzfeld's (1987) study on projections in Mediterranean anthropology gave me a better understanding of the contradictions I had had to live with when doing my fieldwork in southern Italy. The Mediterranean for a long time seems to have been something like an imaginary 'bridge' between what Europeans like to call 'primitive' and 'civilized': Mediterranean cultures are sometimes held to be direct precursors of modern civilization. In this case, living (Christian) Mediterranean peoples are held to be a kind of vanguard in the war against Oriental despotism. Other authors depict 'Mediterranean peasants' as survivals of less accepted aspects of antiquity, as living 'out of time' (Fabian 1983; Thomas 1989) as does any other 'primitive'. The connections of these ambivalences with Mediterranean and world politics have yet to be understood. It is not too surprising, however, that in the era of the Gulf War, Herzfeld's critique of a pan-Mediterranean primitivism was a big success while the same critique uttered in the 1950s by an Italian anthropologist (de Martino 1959) largely fell on deaf ears.

3 For being enabled to make these observations I am indebted to the Tübingen school of German ethnology (*Volkskunde*, folklore, 'Empirische Kulturwissenschaft'), which makes a special point of studying processes of 'folklorization' of customs (see Dow and Lix-

feld 1985). A similar approach was developed by Hobsbawm and Ranger (1983) only at the beginning of the eighties, in the context of Anglo-American historical anthropology and social history.

4 Boissevain (1977) more than a decade ago announced that the 'saints' were 'marching out' in modernizing Malta and then (1984) had the courage to admit that recently there had been a revival of popular religion, partly in folklorized form.

5 This nicely fits anthropological discussions of fieldwork as a manipulative, co-operative process in the course of which 'facts' are 'made' by informants and anthropologist alike (see Rabinow 1977; Tedlock 1979).

6 What historians of literature have vaguely called the reader's *Geistesbeschäftigung* (Jolles 1968 [1930]), his or her 'activity of mind', in the anthropological context is going to become an entirely new field of inquiry into culturally determined forms of processing written symbols (Goody 1987).

7 For a similar concept of the historicity and function of the cults of saints in southern Europe, see Di Tota (1981) and Christian (1972).

8 Theories of contagious magic and *do ut des*, the concept of giving and taking projected into the realm of the supernatural, seem to be pure academic imaginings. Anthropological fieldwork has never produced a single case justifying that kind of generalization. Not even in Roman law, from which the formula *do ut des* was borrowed, was it intended to describe the exertion of force by giving gifts; instead it is an early theory about the uncertainties of generalized exchange (see Van der Leeuw 1933: 327ff.; Krueger 1959: 152; Kaser 1975: 419).

9 Christian (1984) describes similar but politically antagonistic forms of a political and popular Catholicism. The fight against clerical political Catholicism sometimes forced the political left to ignore the political potential inherent in popular Catholic feasts, visions, and the like. In southern Italy I have found no hint of political parties' actively supporting and manipulating the spontaneous 'red' popular Catholicism.

10 In the eighties the development of the St. Donatus parish in Blue Island (Illinois) seems to have been less successful, according to return migrants.

11 Burke (1970: 7–10) similarly describes religion as tautologically founded language and language as an abstraction, that is, something 'supernatural'.

12 Or, as the French 'new' historian Le Roy Ladurie (1979) has put it, in the popular feast can be observed a mixture of individual and social motivations that forces the student to combine Freudian and Durkheimian perspectives.

13 Among more or less conventional historians of literature (Auerbach 1982 [1946]; Jolles 1968 [1930]: 36ff.; Propp 1975) as well as among modern discourse analysts (Burke 1970: 183ff.) and folklorists (Bausinger 1986: 144; Ginzburg 1990: 301), culture is held to be a system of imitation and variation of a few fundamental types of expression.

14 Fieldwork can be seen as a 'passion', an imitation of other ways of experiencing the world, and a form of being possessed by the *heteros*, the cultural 'other'. This idea, long and justifiably rejected as part of a romantic and colonialist attitude towards the exotic (see, e.g., Kramer 1985), has recently been reinterpreted by Lewis (1986: 12) and Kramer (1984) as an essential moment in the process of exploring 'indigenous psychologies' (Heelas and Lock 1981).

15 Galt (1974) employs these terms to distinguish clientelism from the state. My transposition of this dualism to the realm of the supernatural may point to the way in which I worked to transform functionalist, materialist anthropology into a revival of idealist approaches.

16 The development of Mediterranean anthropology can be interpreted as a continuous flux of idealistic and materialistic perspectives. Adherents of the idealistic branch stress the influence of ideas on social realities, the conservatism of communities, and cultural continuity (Peristiany 1966; Pitt-Rivers 1977; Blok and Driessen 1984) while their adversaries point at socioeconomic factors, the regional and national embeddedness of communities, and change (Boissevain and Friedl 1975; Davis 1977; Silverman 1985). As John Davis once put it (personal communication), the modern Mediterranean anthropology of the seventies started with an interest in wickedness, while the new generation of fieldworkers in the eighties is again interested in holiness. But it is not always so easy to discern these types of Mediterranean anthropology in particular persons or generations. There have been retreats from a materialist to a structuralist position (Blok 1981) and some admissions of contradictions (Boissevain 1984), and there have even been authors like White (1980: 3ff., 129–38), who in one Italian village took the inhabitants' idealistic assumptions about their behaviour as reality ('partisans') and in the neighbouring village analysed local political rhetoric as a mere camouflage of bitter socioeconomic realities ('patrons'). These are ambivalent, not to say confused, positions on the part of anthropologists that have nothing to do with the ambivalence on the part of the informants attributed by Gilmore (1982) to Mediterranean cultures.

REFERENCES

Auerbach, Erich (1982 [1946]) *Mimesis*: *Dargestellte Wirklichkeit in der abendländischen Literatur*, München: Beck.

Bausinger, Hermann (1986 [1961] *Volkskultur in der technischen Welt*, Frankfurt: Campus.

Belmont, Nicole (1979) *Arnold Van Gennep: The Creator of French Ethnography*, Chicago: University of Chicago Press.

Berger, Peter (1967) *The Sacred Canopy*, Garden City: Doubleday.

Blok, Anton (1981) 'Rams and billy-goats: a key to the Mediterranean code of honour', *Man*, n.s., 16: 427–40.

Blok, Anton, and Driessen, Henk (eds) (1984) *Cultural Dominance in the Mediterranean Area*, Nijmegen: University of Nijmegen Press.

Boelscher, Marianne (1988) *The Curtain Within: Haida Social and Mythical Discourse*, Vancouver: University of British Columbia Press.

Boissevain, Jeremy (1977) 'When the saints go marching out: reflections on the decline of patronage in Malta', in E. Gellner and J. Waterbury (eds) *Patrons and Clients in Mediterranean Societies*, London: Duckworth.

—— (1984) 'Ritual escalation in Malta', in E. Wolf (ed.) *Religion, Power, and Protest in Local Communities: The Northern Shore of the Mediterranean*, Berlin and New York: Mouton.

Boissevain, Jeremy, and Friedl, John (eds) (1975) *Beyond the Community: Social Process in Europe*, The Hague: Department of Education and Science.

Bronzini, Giovanni Battista (1982) *Cultura contadina e idea meridionalistica*, Bari: Dedalo.

Burke, Kenneth (1970) *The Rhetoric of Religion*, Berkeley: University of California Press.

Christian, William (1972) *Person and God in a Spanish Valley*, New York: Academic Press.

—— (1984) 'Tapping and defining new power: the first months of vision at Ezquioga, July 1931, in A. Blok and H. Driessen (eds) *Cultural Dominance in the Mediterranean Area*, Nijmegen: University of Nijmegen Press, pp. 122–72.

Clifford, James, and Marcus, George (1986) *Writing Culture: The Poetics and Politics of Ethnography*, Berkeley: University of California Press.

Davis, John (1977) *People of the Mediterranean*, London: Routledge and Kegan Paul.

de Martino, Ernesto (1948) *Il mondo magico*, Torino: Boringhieti.

—— (1959) *Sud e magia*, Milan: Il saggiatore.

—— (1977) *La fine del mondo: Contributo all'analisi delle apocalissi culturali*, ed. Clara Gallini, Torino: Einaudi.

Devereux, Georges (1950) 'Catastrophic reactions in normals', *American Imago* 7: 343–49.

—— (1983) 'Weltzerstörung in Wahn und Wirklichkeit', in R. Gehlen and B. Wolf (eds) *Der gläserne Zaun: Aufsätze zu Hans Peter Duerrs 'Traumzeit'*, Frankfurt: Syndikat.

Di Tota, Mia (1981) 'Saint cult and political alignments in southern Italy', *Dialectical Anthropology* 5: 317–29.

Dow, James, and Lixfeld, Hannjost (1985) *German Volkskunde: A Decade of Theoretical Information, Debate, and Reorientation*, Bloomington: Indiana University Press.

Dupré, Georges (1985) *Les naissances d'une société: Espace et historicité chez les Beembé du Congo*, Paris: ORSTOM.

Fabian, Johannes (1983) *Time and the Other: How Anthropology Makes Its Object*, New York: Columbia University Press.

Gallini, Clara (1988) 'Arabesque: images of a myth', *Cultural Studies* 32, 2: 168–80.

—— (1989) 'L'ethnologie italienne: un itinéraire, entretien entre Clara Gallini e Giordana Charuty', *Terrain* 12: 110–24.

Galt, Anthony (1974) 'Rethinking patron-client relationships: the real system and the official system in southern Italy', *Anthropological Quarterly* 47: 182–202.

Gilmore, David (1982) 'Anthropology of the Mediterranean area', *Annual Review of Anthropology* 11: 175–205.

Ginzburg, Carlo (1990) *Hexensabbat: Entzifferung einer nächtlichen Geschichte*, Berlin: Wagenbach.

Goody, Jack (1987) *The Interface between the Written and the Oral*, Cambridge: Cambridge University Press.

Greeley, Andrew (1972) *Unsecular Man: The Persistence of Religion*, New York: Schocken Books.

Hauschild, Thomas (1985) 'Mein Mezzogiorno: Religionsethnoplogische Feldarbeit in Süditalien', in H. Fischer (ed.) *Feldforschungen: Berichte zur Einführung in Probleme und Methoden*, Berlin: Wagenbach.

—— (1986) 'Protestantische Pilger und katholische Körperschaften: Süditalienethnographie zwischen Imagination und Realität', *Zeitschrift für Volkskunde* 82: 19–43.

—— (1987) 'Identità lucana nell'esperienza di un'antropologo culturale', in R. Rosa (ed.) *Identità e specificità di una regione: La Basilicata*, Documentazione Regione 12, Potenza.

—— (1990) 'Studien zum religiösen Diskurs in Süditalien', MS, Köln.

Heelas, Paul, and Lock, Andrew (eds) (1981) *Indigenous Psychologies: The Anthropology of the Self*, London: Academic Press.

Herzfeld, Michael (1987) *Anthropology through the Looking Glass: Critical Ethnography in the Margins of Europe*, Cambridge: Cambridge University Press.

Hobsbawm, Eric, and Ranger, Terence (eds) (1983) *The Invention of Tradition*, Cambridge: Cambridge University Press.

Jolles, André (1968) [1930] *Einfache Formen*, Tübingen: Mohr.

Kantorowicz, Ernst (1965) 'Gods in uniform', in *Selected Studies*, Locust Valley: J. J. Augustin.

Kaser, Max (1975) *Das römische Privatrecht*, vol. 2, *Die nachklassischen Entwicklungen*, München: Beck.

Kenny, Michael (1960) 'Patterns of patronage in Spain', *Anthropological Quarterly* 33: 14–23.

Kramer, Fritz (1977) *Verkehrte Welten: Zur imaginären Ethnographie des 19. Jahrhunderts*, Frankfurt: Syndikat.

—— (1984) 'Notizen zur Ethnologie der Passiones', in E. W. Müller (ed.) *Ethnologie als Sozialwissenschaft*, Kölner Zeitschrift fur Soziologie und Sozialpsychologie 26.

—— (1985) 'Empathy: reflections on the history of ethnology in pre-fascist Germany: Herder, Creuzer, Bachofen, Bastian, and Frobenius', *Dialectical Anthropology* 9: 337–47.

—— (1989) 'The influence of the classical tradition on anthropology and exoticism', in M. Harbsmeier and M. T. Larsen (eds) *The Humanities between Art and Science*, Copenhagen: Akademisk Forlag.

Krueger, Paul (ed.) (1959) *Corpus Iuris Civilis*, Berlin: Weidmann.

Le Roy Ladurie, Emmanuel (1979) *Le Carnaval de Romans*, Paris: Gallimard.

Lewis, Ioan (1986) *Religion in Context: Cults and Charisma*, Cambridge: Cambridge University Press.

Lützenkirchen, Guglielmo (1981) *Mal di Luna*, Rome: Newton Compton.

Peristiany, John G. (ed.) (1966) *Honour and Shame: The Values of Mediterranean Society*, London: Weidenfeld and Nicolson.

Pitt-Rivers, Julian (1954) *The People of the Sierra*, Chicago: University of Chicago Press.

—— (1977) *The Fate of Shechem, or, The Politics of Sex*, Cambridge: Cambridge University Press.

Propp, Vladimir (1975) [1928] *Morphologie des Märchens*, Frankfurt: Suhrkamp.

Rabinow, Paul (1977) *Reflections on Fieldwork in Morocco*, Berkeley: University of California Press.

Richter, Dieter (1985) *Viaggiatori stranieri nel Sud*, Amalfi: Ente Provinciale di Turismo.

Rizzs, Don (1981) *History of Saint Donatus Parish, Blue Island, Ill*, privately printed.

Schramm, Raimund (1988) *Symbolische Logik in der mündlichen Tradition der Aymaras*, Berlin: Dietrich Reimer.

Silverman, Sydel (1985) 'Towards a political economy of the Italian competitive festivals', *Ethnologia Europea* 15: 95–105.

Tedlock, Dennis (1979) 'The analogical tradition and the emergence of a dialogical anthropology', *Journal of Anthropological Research* 35: 387–400.

Thomas, Nicholas (1989) *Out of Time: History and Evolution in Anthropological Discourse*, Cambridge: Cambridge University Press.

Van der Leeuw, Gerardus (1933) *Phänomenologie der Religion*, Tübingen: Mohr.

Van Gennep, Arnold (1943) *Manuel de folklore français contemporain*, vol. 1, *Introduction générale*, Paris: A. Picard.

Vansina, Jan (1965) *Oral Tradition: A Study in Historical Methodology*, trans. H. M. Wright, London: Routledge and Kegan Paul.

Weber, Max (1920) *Gesammelte Aufsätze zur Religionssoziologie*, Tübingen: Mohr.

White, Caroline (1980) *Patrons and Partisans: A Study of Politics in Two Southern Italian Comuni*, Cambridge: Cambridge University Press.

Chapter 3

The gods of the Gentiles are demons

The problem of pagan survivals in European culture

João de Pina-Cabral

In the *nihil obstat* to the sixteenth-century epic *Os Lusíadas*, the inquisitor stresses that, although Camões writes of pagan gods, this should be taken strictly as poetic licence, 'preserving always the truth of our holy faith, that all the gods of the Gentiles are demons' (Camões 1931 [1572]: xxxviii, my translation). This sentence has fascinated me ever since I first came across it. Did it imply that the Holy Inquisition believed that pagan gods *really* existed – that is, that they were true demons? In fact, as I discovered later, this was no invention of Frey Bertholameu Ferreira; it had been Church policy ever since the fourth century, when Eusebius, the archbishop of Caesarea, expounded it in his *Praeparatio Evangelica*.[1]

Of course, we know that there is never a single truth; as Paul Veyne puts it, 'the plurality of modalities of belief is in reality the plurality of the criteria for truth' (1988: 113). Thus, theological monotheism does not require the absolute denial of the existence of other gods; it merely requires a shift in the definition of the notion of divinity. Simply denying the veracity of a series of beliefs, practices, and rituals would not have been sufficient to eradicate them. People's belief does not depend on strict empirical validation, and, even if it did, Christians would find themselves as capable as non-Christians of empirically demonstrating the validity of their practices and beliefs.

The Church, then, declared that those who followed pagan practices were not dealing in mere delusion – that pagan gods really *did* have power, but it was a destructive one. Those forces which had been the very basis of the symbolic construction of the social order ('the morality of the tribe', to use Veyne's [1988: 113] expression) now became enemies of the new order. A phantasmagoric anti-order was constructed, and upon its ruins the true order was raised.[2]

Another central aspect of this process is the denial of 'reason' to things labelled 'pagan' – a denial characteristically enshrined in the notion of 'superstition'. Whether a belief or ritual is reasonable or not depends, however, not on logic alone but also on the very premises used to judge it, that is, on the law. For example, in his commentary on Eusebius's history, Alfonso Tostado, the brilliant fifteenth-century Castilian theologian, says of the Amazons:

> it was reasonable that they should not have lasted for ever, for they took up a way of living against reason and against nature, for God ordered woman and man to be together, not only in bodily coupling in order to reproduce, but especially to live together. . . . They further went against natural reason by wishing to escape from the yoke which God had placed upon them in the day in which man and woman were made, thus saying God to woman, 'Sub viri potestate eris'. That is, you will be under the power of the male or of the husband.
>
> (Tostado 1506–7: fol. lxxvi, my translation)

This passage points to yet another interesting characteristic of things 'pagan': their perpetually impending demise. As they are against reason, these beliefs, practices, and rituals are seen as atavistic, anachronistic, and constantly threatened with disappearance. Judging from the northern Portuguese material that I will discuss presently, however, their resilience seems to match their apparent fragility.

In approaching the problem of this uncanny capacity for survival, I shall start by discussing the relevance of the question to social anthropology today. I shall then continue by considering evidence that, since the Christianization of northern Portugal fourteen centuries ago, there has been a surprising similarity in the areas in which the Church has found people falling into error. I shall argue that this long-term continuity cannot be explained by any single factor, and I shall examine in this light the resurgence in Portugal over the past sixteen years of heterodox religious practices.

MODERN ANTHROPOLOGY AND BLINDNESS TO CONTINUITY

To a Europeanist anthropologist today, the question of pagan survivals may not appear to be very relevant. After all, it would seem, the days in which frightened missionaries and administrators violently destroyed the ritual paraphernalia of pagan cults do seem to be over. However, I believe that it throws light on something which has become so widespread in European culture that we hardly notice it, that is, the claim that certain beliefs, practices, and rituals are survivals from earlier, 'pagan' times. The list of things that one finds classified as 'pagan' in the ethnographic and theological literature on European folk religion is baffling.

Because of what Needham has called 'the intellectualist bent of modern anthropology' (1978: 66),[3] the ethnographies of most trained social anthropologists over the past thirty years have shown a strong concern with discovering the 'reason' – or, better, to use Jane Schneider's (1990: 24) expression, the 'philosophical concern' – behind what our immediate ancestors in folklore or ethnology called 'pagan superstitions'. This I consider to have been one of the major advances in Europeanist anthropology.

Curiously, however, references to pre-Christian survivals, timid though they be, continue to surface regularly (e.g., Badone 1990: 18), and authors implicitly assume that the doctrinal differences which have characterized the relationship between what they call 'folk' or 'popular' religion and Church doctrine arise from these survivals. Furthermore, explanations of sociocultural regional differentiation in terms of the settlement of pre-Christian tribes – be they the Celts, the Saxons, the Swabians, or the Moors – are implicitly accepted. Thus, even though they usually avoid the sort of historicist arguments which earlier ethnologists favoured, the fact is that modern anthropologists too have invested many of the practices and beliefs they encounter with 'pastness' (cf. Martins 1974 and Pina-Cabral 1987). Indeed, at times it is difficult to avoid doing so (consider, e.g., the similarities between pre-Christian *ex votos* in terracotta and the sort of wax *ex voto* that is still so common throughout southern Europe). The problem is that in doing so they are, on the one hand, denying the present appositeness (in symbolic, logical, or sociological terms) of the items they treat as survivals and, on the other, because they implicitly hold to the belief in the value of progress, evaluating them as negative or at least retrograde.

It is to Jane Schneider's credit that she has recently attempted to approach this issue head-on. Her main argument is that

> through a succession of reform movements, of which the Prot-estant Reformation was but the most thorough, literate clerics and preachers of Western Christianity progressively demon-ized European peasant animism, assimilating beliefs in earth spirits and spirits of the dead to a concept of ontological evil and then, after the Enlightenment, denying the existence of these spirits altogether.
>
> (Schneider 1990: 24)

Somewhat following Weber's lead, she draws out an opposition between salvationism and animism, which she defines as 'a set of beliefs and associated rituals according to which the world is permeated by the ghosts and the ancestors of humans and ani-mals and by humanlike spirits that dwell in the objects and forces of the earth' (p. 27).

This is not the place to discuss her argument at length. Suffice it to say that I find this opposition unsatisfactory.[4] To what extent, when we consider the manifestations which she calls ani-mism, are we dealing with a demonstrably specific body of beliefs? Haven't some of them (e.g., St. Anthony's sermon to the fish) been integrated into Catholicism, Judaism, or Islam in one form or another? To what extent are they specifically 'peas-ant' beliefs? For example, has there ever been a period in Europe when astrology or the belief in the curative value of fountains was not present among both the élites and the masses? To say that animism is based on a rural outlook on the world – a deeper contact with the earth, a sense of distributive justice – is to forget that the urban, modern masses evince many of the practices and beliefs which are traditionally classified as animistic. Rather, I want to argue that we cannot compare salvationism with ani-mism, for, while the first is a clearly distinctive phenomenon, the latter is a residual category. By this I mean that, except for brief periods of heightened puritanism in numerically limited social contexts, all societies evince in one form or another some aspect of what Schneider calls animism.

Now, modern anthropology has no language for dealing with these continuities, similarities, recurrences. Part of this is to be blamed on our famous synchronicist bias, but there is more to it. As Hermínio Martins has pointed out, the social sciences of recent decades have been characterized by a prevalence of 'caesurism', that is, theories and concepts which 'stress discontinuity in change as the privileged "moment" of our experience and reflexive cognition of it' (1974: 280). This means that we devalue evidences of relative invariance. The fact, however, is that they loom in the shadows. One of the effects of the increased dialogue between historians and anthropologists and between these two and psychoanalysts is that these evidences are beginning to become unavoidable. In particular, as anthropologists start moving out of the ruralist ghetto and discovering that urban life does not conform to modernist stereotypes the problem of recurrence resurfaces.

FOURTEEN CENTURIES OF SIMILARITIES

In order to make my point I will consider the history of 'pagan' beliefs in northwestern Portugal. The relatively shallow Christianization of Iberian populations during the Roman occupation was countered by the barbaric invasions. The Swabians (or Suebi) occupied northwestern Iberia in 411. Soon after, in 464, they were Christianized by a certain bishop Ajax of the Arian persuasion. This meant that the occupying military élite was Arian, the Romanized aborigines were mostly Catholic, and the rural populations were rather left to themselves with a mixture of local beliefs, Roman pagan beliefs, and perhaps some shreds of Christianity. The situation was finally regularized in 559, when King Teodomiro was converted to Catholicism together with all of his subjects by a man who came to be known as St. Martin of Dume (cf. Maciel 1980).

A native of Pannonia (in today's Hungary), Martin was himself a Swabian, and he undertook with great energy the task of integrating this Swabian kingdom in the far west into the Roman Church. He left us a series of writings, mostly dealing, as is to be expected, with liturgical matters. Among these, three documents have proved particularly interesting to ethnologists: the canons of the two councils of Braga, which are held to have been mostly written under his supervision, and a sermon aiming at correcting the errors of rural people, his famous 'Sermo De Correctione Rusticorum', written in a more vulgar form of Latin in order, we presume, to be more widely understood. In both instances, we encounter listings of errors, superstitions, and pagan survivals which should be abandoned. In the case of the canons, we even find references to the fact that priests participated in some of these errors. The text of the sermon was written under the inspiration of the 'Sermo De Catechizandis Rudibus' of St. Augustine and was very influential throughout Europe; we know of its use in France and southern Germany in the seventh and eighth centuries, respectively, and in England at the end of the tenth.

In a valuable article written in 1957, Luis Chaves, a devoutly Catholic ethnologist, sets down a list of these 'rustic superstitions', comparing them with a further list encountered in the constitutions of the dioceses of Braga and Oporto, produced in 1639 and 1687, respectively, and, finally, with his own findings in the same region during the 1950s. He expressly states that he was a witness to the end of this traditional culture (1957: 253). Today, however, we know that the most radical changes in the rural culture and society of the northwest actually took place ten to fifteen years after him. In any case, twenty years later I was to find in the Alto Minho most of the 'rural superstitions' that he claimed to date from pre-Christian times (Pina-Cabral 1986; 1987). (As I have said, one of the interesting characteristics of the temporal mirage of pagan survivals is that they are seen as constantly on the verge of disappearing.) The question is, Are these similarities surprising?

Chaves starts with St. Martin's references to the 'cult of heavenly bodies' – magical practices related to the sun, the moon, and the stars – and finds that the seventeenth-century constitutions refer specifically to praying to the moon and the stars and to the prediction of future events and that a long list of symbolic beliefs and practices on this topic has survived to his own time (cf. Pina-Cabral 1986: 119–24).

The next item is what he calls the 'cult of fire'. The constitutions do not speak of it, but we presume that practices dealing with fire and especially the hearth continued because they are very widespread in the twentieth century. The same can be said of the 'cult of water' and various forms of purification through water, which the constitutions only hint at. Then comes the 'cult of the dead' and particularly the attempt to speed the passage of the deceased from the world of the living to that of the dead;

this is present in all three sources. The same is the case with the next item, the 'cult of nature', a varied collection of beliefs dealing with stones, waters, trees, mountains, etc.

Then comes a series of items dealing with circular time, particularly lucky days, hours, and moments of the year. The next group of items deals with prediction of the future by reference to the behaviour of birds or humans and by means of other forms of divination (he includes here beliefs about the right and the left side). Another series covers modes of holding evil forces at bay: prayers, amulets, exorcisms, etc. In one form or another, of course, these too are present in all three sources, as well as a group of items dealing with sorcery through the use of formulae, herbs, and other substances.

Three items in Chaves's list deserve specific attention. St. Martin refers to the cult of pagan deities, but these are absent from both the seventeenth-century constitutions and Chaves's own list. In exchange, both of them make much of the cult of the Devil, to which St. Martin had not specifically referred, perhaps because the gods of the Gentiles were his demons.

Curiously, whilst both the other two sources refer to the fact that some priests were known to participate in superstitious rituals, Chaves claims that this is 'out of the question' in his time (1957: 263). Considering what we know today about the collaboration of priests in heterodox practices (cf. Pina-Cabral 1986; Brettell 1990; Taylor 1990), this statement reflects either Chaves's unwillingness to recognize something he abhorred or the fact that, in those days of greater religious repression, such acts were less apparent.

Three themes, however, are absent from both of the earlier sources which Chaves cannot but include: the magical use of numbers (namely, two, three, five, seven, and thirteen [cf. Needham 1978: 10]), the whole complex of beliefs related to naming, and, finally, an item he calls 'monsters', in which he includes witches, werewolves, enchanted Mooresses, etc. Do we deduce that such beliefs were not present in the days of St. Martin? Much as does Chaves himself, we know that they were. In fact, as far as witches and werewolves are concerned we have another good source – Tostado, who, in the fifteenth century, discusses with the empirical curiosity and open-mindedness characteristic of those pre-Inquisitional days a case of a self-acknowledged *bruxa*, a woman who claimed to fly to great distances after rubbing her naked body with oily substances (1506–7: fol. c verso). Her body was branded with a red-hot iron during her trance in order to test whether she was faking, and it was concluded that she was not because she felt the burns only after emerging from it. Even though, in her case, it was apparent to him that she 'did not do anything by deeds but only by thoughts', he still claimed that 'we cannot conclude from this that those women whom they call witches do not at times pass from one place to another, causing damage'.

It seems doubtful that any ethnographer who has done fieldwork in Europe or, for that matter, anywhere else will be at all surprised by the contents of Chaves's list. But why, then, have we no analytical language to cope with such phenomena? Much as we are haunted by repetition, recurrence, fixity, and continuation in cultural behaviour, our fascination with the cognitive value of change – our 'caesurism' – leads us to push these aspects into the shadows.

FIXITY AND RECURRENCE

The categories that Chaves chooses are probably not those we would choose today. Indeed, his exercise suffers from many problems, perhaps the main one being his whole-hearted acceptance of the Church's logic. This is a list of things which the Church countered, but he is the first to acknowledge that the Church has always worked with 'archetypes', which, in his words, 'she brings from the depth of the centuries to the symbolic truth of liturgy' (1957: 254, my translation). The reason Chaves has to alter his logic, including items such as 'monsters' and the magical use of numbers in his list when they are not to be found in the two earlier sources, is not that people earlier on did not hold these beliefs but rather that the Church then held them to be true. In the seventeenth century people were being tortured and burned at the stake for being witches or for practising cabalistic exercises.

Do we then assume that, much like their impending demise, this sameness of pagan survivals is a mirage? I will answer this with Tostado's conclusions about witches: 'Some are true and some are false . . . and not all the false ones are of the same type, nor do all the true ones arise from the same source' (1506–7: fol. c verso, my translation). In other words, the question is complex and cannot be reduced to a single issue. Thus, without claiming to be exhaustive, I want to identify two constitutive aspects in particular, as I believe their confusion is partly responsible for the puzzling nature of these phenomena. Both of these have recently been identified by anthropological theorists, and I will therefore borrow their terminologies, hoping that I do not distort their ideas out of recognition.

First, we have phenomena akin to what Maurice Bloch has called 'ritual fixity'. Briefly, in his study of Merina circumcision ritual over the past 200 years, Bloch (1986) came across what he considered a rather surprising stability in the symbolic structure of the ritual. Even though political and economic conditions had altered very radically, this ritual seemed to have continued to be useful to the Merina, which suggested that the question of the determination of ritual by ideology could not be approached in a simplistic way. The same ritual, it would seem, could serve different masters. As he put it, 'political dominators put on a mantle that has been worn by different types of dominators before them, they do not make this mantle anew' (1986: 191). This is possible, according to him, only because rituals are neither actions nor statements; 'they are not means of communicating but rather of expressing' (1986: 177).

Fixity, then, would explain the continuation of ritual practices far beyond the life of the specific conditions within which they were wrought. But does this apply only to ritual? Does it not also apply to uses of spatial structures (for example, house types or holy places in landscape) and even of some texts? For instance, the survival of proverbs can only be understood in this way. In Portugal, many of those current today were already being used in mediaeval times (Mattoso 1984; Arriscado Nunes et al. 1989). I suggest, therefore, that fixity is a characteristic of culture that should be further researched.

The second aspect is entirely different. According to Rodney Needham, the reason a list such as Chaves's cannot be surprising to any ethnographer is that all cultures manifest a series of 'capacities, proclivities and constraints that universally make up human nature' (1978: 8). What he calls 'primary factors' are simple imaginative resources that all human beings use in the construction of their imaginative universes. They may be abstract (such as binary opposition or transition) or perceptual (such as the use of colours, textures, etc.), and their number is limited.

These factors may be 'differentially synthesized into distinct com-
plexes representing disparate social concerns' (1978: 42). These
synthetic images or archetypes are identifiable, for they too are
present in many cultures. The case Needham chooses to exemp-
lify his argument is that of the image of the witch.

An argument of this sort allows us to return to phenomena of
cultural continuity with less uneasiness. Indeed, how can we
accept the suggestion that, even though they are 'meaningless'
aspects of culture, belief in the healing power of fountains or
the divinatory power of birds or even the fear of witches or
werewolves should have continued to be so gripping to most
people in Portugal after fourteen centuries?

An example of the sort of tight corner that one can find oneself
in because of a failure to recognize that there are recurrent
aspects of culture is Jorge Dias's explicit surprise over the custom
of using open umbrellas in marriage processions in Vilarinho da
Furna, one of the mountain communities he studied. I stress that
his surprise must here be seen as a measure of his astuteness as
a sociological observer and not the contrary. He comments in a
footnote:

> We know of the same custom in . . . Serra de Montemuro.
> It is not likely that this habit would have been common in
> other regions of the country, having then taken refuge in these
> more archaic regions, for folding umbrellas cannot have long
> existed among such people. We must see here a simple
> phenomenon of convergence. . . . The umbrella is usually
> considered by country people . . . as a sign of elegance and
> distinction. . . . Even though the folding umbrella is recent
> . . . the use of umbrellas for the sun is ancient and still today
> is an attribute of dignity in various Islamic countries and in
> Abyssinia.
>
> (Dias 1981 [1948]: 183–4, my translation)

But recurrence has to be associated with fixity if we are to
develop an anthropological approach to temporal similarity.
Although the two aspects operate in logically distinct forms, they
are jointly brought to bear on the same cultural practices. This,
then, would allow us to make sense of the reappearance of
forgotten features of the circumcision ritual on which Bloch
reports or the exceptionally acute memory which elders demonstrate when they are questioned in the context of the ritual (1986:

166, 167). This type of reinvention within a context of ritual fixity must be seen as distinct from the simple recurrence of Needham's primary factors or synthetic images. As it occurs within previously set limits, it is largely responsible for the sort of regional identity through time which Europeanist ethnology has traditionally accounted for by references to Celtic, Swabian, or Moorish ancestry.

THE FUTURE OF SUPERSTITION

The often expressed conviction that, over the past century, the spread of formal education, the mass media, and consumerism has resulted in the abandonment of the sort of beliefs, practices, and rituals which we have been considering is also, I think, a consequence of the mirage of pagan survivals. I will consider briefly two Portuguese examples: the cult surrounding the supposed grave of a black slave near Oporto and contact with the recently deceased through the use of mediums.

Throughout western Europe, there is a whole complex of beliefs, legends, and cults surrounding the image of the man who, being innocent, was wrongly sentenced to death or even executed. This complex is ancient in northwestern Iberia, where it has often been associated with the shrine of St. James of Compostela and the figure of the roasted cock that sings (cf. Pires de Lima 1963: 55–74; Meyer 1970: 41–68). An interesting instance of this complex is the cult that surrounds the grave of a black man in Gemunde, Maia, on the outskirts of the city of Oporto. Legend has it that, sometime around the end of the eighteenth century, this slave, accused by his master of a crime he had not committed, was tied to the tail of a horse and dragged to death. He is supposed to have been buried on the spot where he died and where, ever since, there has been a little shrine.

The Church has systematically opposed this cult, arguing that there is no grave there and no proof that such a man was holy or even existed. In 1841, at the instance of the bishop of Oporto, the district administrator, accompanied by other civil authorities, a representative of the bishop, and a group of soldiers, visited the place, destroyed the shrine, and took away the stones that covered the supposed grave. Having dug all over, they found no evidence of there ever having been a burial on the spot. The continuation of the cult was banned in the most definite terms, and the Church went to the extent of organizing a religious festivity in the parish church on the same day as the 'black man's' annual celebration in order to discourage people from participating in it (Pires de Lima 1949: 51).

A century later, Pires de Lima expressed surprise that this cult had survived and that its annual *festa* had lost none of its vigour. What is perhaps more surprising, considering that in the meantime this rural parish has been integrated into the sphere of influence of Greater Oporto, is that in the 1980s the *festa* is still going strong.

The second example is a series of beliefs, practices, and rituals related to the attempt to safeguard the passage of the recently deceased from the world of the living to that of the dead. This is accompanied by the belief that these dead people can cause misfortune if they left behind unresolved problems in their relations with the living (cf. Pina-Cabral 1986). Over the past few decades, there has developed in Portuguese cities an enormous network of mediums who, through the help of powerful spirit guides, can contact these deceased persons, talk in their voices, and express their wishes to their surviving relatives. These spirit guides, the souls of persons of great spiritual power, protect the mediums from evil spirits and demonic influences. (It is possible that, in their more recent aspects, these practices have been influenced by the Spiritualist movement.) The three spirit guides which seem most used throughout Portugal are Father Cruz, a charismatic priest who lived in the middle of our century, Sousa Martins, a professor of medicine who lived at the turn of the last century and is reported to have been particularly devoted to his clients, and Santa Maria Adelaide, a woman whose body did not decay after her death and whose shrine is not under the control of the Church.

My aim is to show that, first, practices of this type are flourishing throughout Portugal and by no means only in rural, backward, or uneducated contexts and, second, that the reason for this is to be found not in the increase of superstition, the loss of real values, or the work of greedy people with evil intentions who are cheating the people, as the Church would have it, but rather in the incapacity of the Church to continue to control people's religious imagination by means of physical force.

I insist on physical force because it is becoming increasingly apparent that, except during brief periods of revolutionary change, the Church in Portugal has always had access to state power. The end of the Inquisition in the eighteenth century was by no means the end of this collaboration. The case of the cult of the black man is an example of this, but other, more recent examples are to hand. Joyce Riegelhaupt, for instance, has written about it (1973), and the history of the collaboration between the Church, the paramilitary police, and the secret police during Salazar's regime is still unwritten. In certain cases, such as the famous Santa da Ladeira do Pinheiro, open battles were fought, with charges by the mounted police and lengthy physical occupation of cult areas.

Since the onset of the democratic regime in 1975, the open use of physical force has been less easy to accomplish, but attempts to do so have not quite ceased. For example, after a lengthy battle for the control of the body of Santa Maria Adelaide, the *freguesia* council (an elected body) managed to outmanoeuvre the Church, and the cult (which is economically immensely profitable) is still expanding. In May 1983, a man went up to the glass case in which the body is kept and, brandishing a heavy hammer, broke the glass and seriously damaged the face and body of the saint. The population went on a rampage, and had the police not quickly succeeded in spiriting the man away he might well have been lynched. Little was heard of him after this, but a year later a small news item in a local newspaper reported that he had left prison and gone to Spain, where he was studying to be a priest (*Comércio do Porto*, 1 January 1984). In the case of Sousa Martins the Church is in the uncomfortable position of having his major place of cult, a statue representing him dressed in academic gown, right in front of the offices of the Patriarch in Lisbon. In 1980, the Church asked the municipality to clear the statue of all the *ex votos* and cult objects which usually surround it, but the attempt failed because of strong popular opposition.

There is no evidence that people's religious imagination has been reduced in modern, urban society. The contexts of belief or, better, the modalities of truth with which we approach these areas of the constitutive imagination may have changed, but the appeal of the old themes seems to have survived. The following story, told to me by a highly placed Portuguese civil servant, helps to illustrate this point: she was born after her father's death. When she was twelve her paternal grandmother, feeling that it was tragic that she had never known him, took the girl to a medium through whom she had regularly spoken with him ever since his death. Through the mouth of the medium the girl heard her father's voice for the first time, and it frightened her deeply. Today she says that she does not believe in these things but that that experience was a formative one in her life. She says that she is afraid to participate in spiritualist seances. As Veyne has put it, 'For my part, I hold ghosts to be simple fictions but perceive their truth nonetheless. I am almost neurotically afraid of them' (1988: 87). How different is this from Tostado's solution to the problem of werewolves? According to him, it was improbable that men could undergo such a metamorphosis, but God and the demons could alter appearances in such a way that everyone who saw the werewolf, including himself and the wolves, thought that he looked like a wolf (1506–7: fol. xcix-c).

This issue raises serious moral questions which we, as anthropologists, have mostly been avoiding. The question of the truthfulness of symbolic classifications and symbolic behaviour is considerably altered if seen from the point of view of recent medical discoveries concerning healing and resistance to disease in the fields of cancer and AIDS research.

CONCLUSION

Too many societies, cultures, and religions hold beliefs in entities such as witches, werewolves, and water sprites and practise things such as sacrifice, lustration, initiation, and augury for these not to be easily recognizable by members of other cultures. The recognition of these similarities, of course, is not based on strict identity but depends on something like what some philosophers call 'interpretative charity' (cf. Godlove 1989). Some such notion is indispensable for anthropologists approaching the task of mapping out similarities in terms of fixity or recurrence, but it is equally essential for the understanding of the capacity which members of distinct 'cultural worlds' evince for recognizing the relevance and power of the practices, rituals, and beliefs of others.

Pagan gods are demons only because, whilst different from our own god, they are recognizably divine. They lack reason because, much in the same way as did the Amazonians for Tostado, they do not conform to the law. Once their 'reason' is denied, however, their persistence becomes mysterious and powerful. It has often been pointed out that human beings invest with an awesome power things which they cannot know (cf. Cohen 1981: 3, citing Simmel). As I have argued elsewhere, some of the social dynamics of religious deviance in the context of Portuguese society depend precisely on the manipulation of this power (Pina-Cabral 1990).[5]

But it must also be understood that the ascription of 'pagan-ness' to these beliefs, practices, and rituals was an *ex post facto* phenomenon. What was different became anterior. Thus, pagan survivals are the products of a struggle for power between the religious creativity of the masses and the Church's need for control – the process so brilliantly examined by Robert Hertz in his work on the cult of St. Besse (1928).

When, in the course of the nineteenth century, the evolution-ists laid out the ground on which anthropology as a discipline was to develop, they had recourse to a similar process of tem-poralization of difference in order to mark the boundary between themselves and their object, the Other (cf. Fabian's study of this process [1983]). The history of the survival to our present day of this image of the primitive society has recently been traced by Kuper (1989). It is an image constituted by two central temporal metaphors: the movement from kinship to territoriality and from status to contract (Pina-Cabral 1989) and the movement from magic to religion and from symbol to reason. In both cases, however, it is becoming increasingly apparent to many anthropol-ogists that these metaphors have become hindrances to under-standing. We are urgently in need of a thoroughgoing critique of the implications for anthropology of the notion of modernity.

NOTES

1 I thank my parents, Daniel and Ana de Pina Cabral, for the generous help they have given me both in terms of discussing these topics and in terms of gathering written information. I must stress, however, that my opinions here expressed do not in any way reflect theirs.
2 We are already familiar with such processes from other contexts (see Bloch and Parry 1982: 218).
3 I understand 'intellectualist' to mean 'doctrine which reduces all physi-cal facts to intellectual facts . . . and, thus, does not recognize the originality and primacy of tendency and affectivity' (Cuvillier 1956).

4 Is it not another version of what Tipps (1973: 212–13) calls the 'tradition–modernity contrast'?

5 I suppose this is what Raymond Smullyan means in the phrase which Umberto Eco uses as an epigraph to his *Foucault's Pendulum*: 'super-stition brings bad luck'.

REFERENCES

Arriscado Nunes, João, Pina-Cabral, João, and Feijó, Rui Graça (1989) 'Familial scenarios: using proverbs in the study of family patterns', paper presented to the 4th International Meeting on Portugal, Durham, NH.

Badone, Ellen (1990) 'Introduction', in E. Badone (ed.) *Religious Orthodoxy and Popular Faith in European Society*, Princeton: Princeton University Press.

—— (ed.) (1990) *Religious Orthodoxy and Popular Faith in European Society*, Princeton: Princeton University Press.

Bloch, Maurice (1986) *From Blessing to Violence: History and Ideology in the Circumcision Ritual of the Merina of Madagascar*, Cambridge: Cambridge University Press.

Bloch, Maurice, and Parry, Jonathan (1982) *Death and the Regeneration of Life*, London: Academic Press.

Brettell, Caroline (1990) 'The priest and his people: the contractual basis for religious practice in rural Portugal', in E. Badone (ed.) *Religious Orthodoxy and Popular Faith in European Society*, Princeton: Princeton University Press.

Camões, Luís de (1931 [1572]) *Os Lusíadas*, facsimile edn, introd. Carolina Michaelis de Vasconcelos, Lisboa: Imprensa Nacional.

Chaves, Luis (1957) 'Costumes e tradições vigentes no século VI e na actualidade', *Bracara Augusta* 3/4.

Cohen, Abner (1981) *The Politics of Elite Culture*, Berkeley: University of California Press.

Cuvillier, Armand (1956) *Vocabulário de Filosofia*, Lisboa: Editorial Gleba.

Dias, Jorge (1981 [1948]) *Vilarinho da Furna*, Lisboa: Imprensa Nacional/Casa da Moeda.

Fabian, Johannes (1983) *Time and the Other: How Anthropology Makes Its Object*, New York: Columbia University Press.

Godlove, Terry F., Jr. (1989) *Religion, Interpretation, and Diversity of Belief: The Framework Model from Kant to Durkheim to Davidson*, Cambridge: Cambridge University Press.

Hertz, Robert (1928) *Mélanges de sociologie réligieuse et folklore*, Paris: Alcan.

Kuper, Adam (1989) *The Invention of Primitive Society*, London: Routledge.

Maciel, Manuel Justino Pinheiro (1980) 'O "De Correctione Rusticorum" de S. Martinho de Dume', *Bracara Augusta* 78 (91).

Martins, Hermínio (1974) 'Time and theory in sociology' in John Rex (ed.) *Approaches to Sociology*, London: Routledge and Kegan Paul.

Mattoso, J. (1984) *O essencial sobre provérbios medievais portugueses*, Lisboa: Imprensa Nacional.

Meyer, Maurits de (1970) 'La légende du pendu – miraculeusement sauvé par Saint Jacques de Compostelle et le témoignage du coq rôti (Galo de Barcelos)', *Revista de Etnografia* 15.

Needham, Rodney (1978) *Primordial Characters*, Charlottesville: University Press of Virginia.

Pina-Cabral, João de (1986) *Sons of Adam, Daughters of Eve: The Peasant Worldview of the Alto Minho*, Oxford: Clarendon Press.

—— (1987) 'Paved roads and enchanted Mooresses: the perception of the past among the peasant population of the Alto Minho', *Man*, n.s., 22: 715–35.

—— (1989) 'L'héritage de Maine', *Ethnologie Française* 19: 329–40.

—— (1990) 'A legitimação da crença: mudança social e bruxas no norte de Portugal', in Fernando Oliveira Baptista *et al.* (eds) *Estudos em Homenagem a Ernesto Veiga de Oliveira*, Lisboa: INIC.

Pires de Lima, Augusto César (1949) 'As lendas', in *Estudos Etnográficos, Filológicos e Históricos*, vol. 4, Porto: Junta de Provincia de Douro Litoral.

Pires de Lima, Fernando de Castro (1963) 'A lenda do Senhor do Galo de Barcelos', *Revista de Etnografia* 1 (1).

Riegelhaupt, Joyce (1973) '*Festas e padres*: the organization of religious action in a Portuguese parish', *American Anthropologist* 75: 835–52.

Schneider, Jane (1990) 'Spirits and the spirit of capitalism', in E. Badone (ed.) *Religious Orthodoxy and Popular Faith in European Society*, Princeton: Princeton University Press.

Taylor, Lawrence J. (1990) 'Stories of power, powerful stories: the drunken priest in Donegal', in E. Badone (ed.) *Religious Orthodoxy and Popular Faith in European Society*, Princeton: Princeton University Press.

Tipps, Dean C. (1973) 'Modernization theory and the comparative study of societies: a critical perspective', *Comparative Studies in Society and History* 15: 199–26.

Tostado, Alfonso (1506–7) *Comento sobre a historia de Euzébio*, pt. 3, Salamanca: Hans Gisser.

Veyne, Paul (1988) *Did the Greeks Believe in Their Myths? An Essay on the Constitutive Imagination*, trans. Paula Wissing, Chicago and London: University of Chicago Press.

Chapter 4

Segmentation and politics in the European nation-state
Making sense of political events

Michael Herzfeld

Segmentation, until recently regarded as characteristic only of stateless societies or at most of societies with a recently developed state structure, should instead be seen as the means whereby competing stories about the past are organized to give credibility to actions in the present and future. After briefly discussing the writings of nationalistic folklorists in Greece, I turn to the conduct of political life on modern Crete – a society that combines agnatic, segmentary kinship *groups* with a bilateral terminology and fierce localism with equally fierce nationalism. I specifically examine the recent debates over government attempts to sequestrate church property and the 1986 municipal elections in a Cretan town.[1] On the basis of these materials, I propose to link the phenomenon of segmentation to the semantics of politically motivated accounts of future and present action and to suggest that this relationship exhibits important similarities to the logic of nationalistic folklore.

EVENTS, SEGMENTS, AND HISTORIES

Why, in elections, do the supporters of an obviously doomed candidacy continue to insist that a surprise victory is on the way? Instead of dismissing this as mere bombast, we should rather entertain the possibility that it has material consequences. Willingly supporting a losing party may not look so stupid a few years later, because the loser may be able to reward that support in unpredictable ways.

All parties are engaged in complicated calculations of benefit and obligation. They make use of history, especially historical precedent, and in so doing they reinforce certain readings of the past that provide the ground on which they can contest newly emergent strategic interests. Against the image of the feckless peasant or small-town resident, I suggest that actors anticipate the limitations of a situation dominated by larger interest groups and figure out clever ways of getting what they want – not necessarily in a crassly material sense but in terms of a highly practical balance of social and material capital. In the social world they inhabit, the position of underdog may be one to compete for while denying that one is an underdog at all.

The argument has two axes, both of them aspects of the rhetorical structures of factuality. On one axis, *time* does not simply pursue a linear progression but becomes a play of ideas about inevitability and the specificity of historical events. On the other, actors alternately contest and reinforce the statist premise of pursuing a unified national goal and sharing a single history.

Because anthropologists are used to thinking in terms of a duality that separates acephalous societies from 'pyramidally' organized ones, they often overlook the *necessarily* segmentary character of virtually all nation-states. As 'imagined communities' (Anderson 1983), nation-states enfold a variety of mutually competing and sometimes incompatible interests. They must reduce each of these to the status of a 'refraction' (Evans-Pritchard 1956) of some fundamental, transcendental 'national character'. At the all-important local levels of action, however, the subdivisions of these unities are conceived in terms no less essentialist (Geertz 1973: 240–1) than that of the encompassing national identity. It was this search for segmentable (and thus unifiable) essential characteristics that gave folklorists such prominence in nineteenth-century European nationalism, as they sought to show that an often bewildering kaleidoscope of cultural difference could be reduced to transcendent oneness (see Herzfeld 1987: 77–81).

Conversely, it was the importance of immediately thereafter *forgetting* the process whereby such unities came into being that then relegated folklore to the sidelines of social science. Once folklore had done its work, it could be marginalized, its role as the indissoluble cement of nationalism pushed firmly into the background. In social anthropology, the word 'folklore' has the musty smell of irrelevance. For many anthropologists, folklore is too embarrassingly linked to Eurocentric nationalism.

Social anthropology, however, has effectively suppressed its own historical contribution to the various European nationalisms. The undeniably important task of winkling out the colonialist underpinnings of much modern anthropology may have inadvertently contributed to that suppression, because it made folklore look marginal by elevating the voices of 'natives' over those of 'peasants' – those domesticated 'others' who have been dragooned into essentialist 'national characters' throughout Europe.

One more complex and important link between anthropology and folklore is the relationship between the concept of 'textual variant' and the idea of segmentation. At one, rather simplistic level, one could argue that textual variation follows the social cleavages of the objective social world. Thus, the more unlike two groups are, the more distant their respective variants of a given text will be. But difference, textual or political, is never just a matter of absolute fact. Thus, in both cases, what we are looking at is the *perception* of similarity and difference, and the connection becomes still clearer when we treat present-day narratives about political action in the same taxonomic framework as 'folk narrative'. Both genres are constructions in their own right, but both are also *constructed* as more or less accurate tokens of a basic type at a more inclusive level of segmentation, whether of folklorists or politicians (or people who are both). Just as variants could be reduced to a single *Urtext*, socially and culturally differentiated sectors of what was often a newly constituted national identity bowed to the centripetal arguments of statism.

What an observer may see as 'merely' variants of a common text will look from the inside like marks of real difference. Because the members of a social group can presume a high degree of shared knowledge, they do not specify the detail that would render their accounts transparent to outsiders – something they rarely want to do (or are regarded as traitors for doing). This produces the effect of nonsense or textual 'corruption' for outsiders, whose view is predicated on assumptions of pure referentiality and precise correlation between text and meaning. For them, each folksong or tale type 'means' one thing only, and all variants are reduced versions of this hypothetical essence rather than meaningful local constructions. This is why nationalist folklorists generally treat texts of obstinately local character as debased and uninformative: they lack the codes needed to read such texts in context. Insiders, by contrast, can 'read in' the details that make the texts locally salient.

My strategy here will be to examine two historical issues to show how the Greek state has co-opted concepts of personhood and agency to its own ends – to the possessive individualism that, as Handler (1988: 6) has argued, characterizes nationalism. This argument is not only compatible with a segmentary view of social relations but indeed depends upon it. It entails a successful translation of social values to the level of cultural truths. Social life in a nation-state framework is in a constant condition of tension as each actor or interest group tries to essentialize a particular set of actions as social facts.

THE LABILITY OF HISTORY: A PRACTICAL EXAMPLE

Anthropologists usually approach history as a negotiable entity (see Appadurai 1981). One of the most elegant arguments in this genre has been Michael Thompson's (1979) demonstration that competing historical narratives exhibit segmentary properties. As he points out, competing versions of history reduce genealogical depth and streamline the past so that it conforms to a more orderly progression.

To this insight we might add here the common phenomenon whereby the apical common ancestor of feuding groups represents a point of idealized, transcendent unity. In modern politics, the same principle holds true. Thus, when the people of the Greek island of Crete compete to identify Eleftherios Venizelos as the ancestor of their particular faction, they are also reproducing a political version of the expulsion from Eden. That narrative figure is, very simply, as follows. In the beginning Crete was autonomous. In that early phase, all was harmony. Then Crete became part of the Greek state, and Venizelos came into his own as a national leader. Gradually, the Venizelist tradition began to subdivide, and its embodiment in radically divergent political parties spelled the end of harmony. This scenario reproduces the central feature of more 'traditional' symbolisms of time: in the long ago, the villagers dwelt in harmonious love – a theological metaphor – which their present fractiousness has ruined forever.

In order to see this symbolism in action, one need not argue that Cretans actually believe in their rival histories. As with sociological theory (Karp and Maynard 1983), segmentation does not automatically overdetermine historical accounts. Rather, a relativity of allegiance, expressed as a system of moral categories, provides the rhetorical point of reference for modes of justifying past conduct or anticipating future action, and the rhetorical games thus generated play a significant role in determining the course of events.

Dresch (1986) has made a persuasive case along these lines and has argued in favor of divorcing segmentation from lineage theory (see also Karp and Maynard 1983; Herzfeld 1987). He suggests that the segmentary categories to be found in certain Middle Eastern societies are temporally and logically antecedent to the events they are invoked to explain and that they partly determine the cultural form of action.

While this is a defensible argument in the context of Yemeni politics, its wider comparative implications call for further, careful exploration. Is segmentation so specific to certain cultures that it gives the forms of action a distinctive commonality? Or is that commonality, which Dresch has demonstrated in widely divergent areas of Yemeni social experience, rather the result of the degree of explicitness with which Yemenis acknowledge segmentary properties? After working in a village in which unilineal kinship played a much larger role than it does in many other parts of Greece and where in consequence people were much more willing to recognize the phenomenon of segmentation, I became much more aware of its appearance in many aspects of Greek life where this particular kinship idiom did not obtain. In his justifiable eagerness to detach segmentation from particular kinship structures, Dresch has perhaps underestimated the extent to which we have all tended to ignore segmentary phenomena in situations where our training may have led us not to expect it.

Only the persistent unitarianism of the modern nation-states that we inhabit prevents us from seeing that segmentation lurks everywhere. Just as Dresch argues that the concept organizing the degrees and levels of segmentary differentiation in Yemeni society is that of honour, moreover, I contend that one cannot understand segmentation independently of the logic of concealment and display. While he seems to treat the phenomenon as exclusive to a certain kind of Middle Eastern society, however, I look for it in all sorts of other places as well. The term 'honour' suggests a degree of cultural specificity that might discourage extraregional comparative study. Thus, while remaining in agreement with Dresch's basic position, I would like to shift the terminology towards something at once more generic ethnographically and more specific structurally. 'Collective selfhood', while less elegant, would seem to fit the bill.

The reasons for this have to do with the predication of shifting concepts of group identity on the one Archimedean spot, oneself. True, the 'content' of 'ego' is never *really* clear. It is in the nature of social experience, however, that collective identities – who 'we' are – is a good deal less so, which I take to be the point of Meeker's (1979: 100) observation that segmentation is a 'metaphor' for the uncertainty of social life. Starting from a relativistic reading of Fernandez's (1974: 120) view of metaphor as a 'sign predicated upon an inchoate subject', we can say that 'we' is always in some sense a metaphor for, as well as a synecdoche of, an illusorily more concrete 'I'.

In Greece, this 'I-ness' is a highly androcentric concept. Not only are national and international conflicts often perceived in terms of agonistic interpersonal relations (e.g., 'the *eghoismos* of the prime ministers') but the very notion of the nation is often expressed as *yenos* (patriline), in formal as well as Classical Greek and etymologically cognate with the Cretan term *yenia*. The intellectual founders of the nation are often called the 'Great Teachers of the *Yenos*'.

Before we proceed to reviewing two cases – the 1986 municipal elections and the nationwide battles over government sequestration of church property a few months later – a brief word about Cretan political history will be helpful. Crete makes an especially interesting locus for the study of these issues because its locally still flamboyant androcentrism and the continuing use of agnatic kinship for many purposes make the segmentary character of events and the uses of agnatic metaphors much more transparent than they usually are elsewhere in Greece. After Greece became nominally autonomous in 1899, a young Khaniot politician, Eleftherios Venizelos, began a rapid rise to local and then national prominence. Elected prime minister of Greece for the first time in 1911, he represented the irredentist goals of ardent nationalism in international affairs with liberalism at home. After the 1922 collapse of the Greek armies in Asia Minor, a calamity in which his political enemies were inculpated to the point of incurring the death penalty, he gained massive support from the flood of Asia Minor refugees who resented both the machinations of the conservatives who had brought that calamity upon them and the horrendous living conditions that the Venizelists promised to alleviate. While some refugees eventually moved still farther to the left, mostly in despair of ever gaining ground under any moderate government beholden to large commercial interests (see Hirschon 1989: 44, 47), the majority continued to support the Venizelist cause. On Crete, this support was swelled by local pride. Venizelos was a local son, his liberalism and anti-monarchism attributes that could easily be assimilated to the androcentric self-stereotype of the freedom-loving Cretan rebel against authority.

It was this same Venizelos who is credited with inventing the rhyming couplet 'If the billy-goat is strong, the sheepfold can't hold him in; a man makes his patrigroup [*yenia*], not the patrigroup the man!' Cretans cite this couplet frequently. In it are fused the Cretanness of the politician who could come up with such an apt utterance, the celebration of a strong relationship between *eghoismos* and an agnatic concept of personhood, and an appropriate measure of self-reference. In addition, Venizelos is the political equivalent of an apical ancestor, a being whose very essence is segmented into party-political refractions in (so to speak) the fractious realities of the present age (Herzfeld 1985: 99). Political acts on Crete are always subject to a sort of Venizelist litmus test. One's enemies' actions are always a violation of the essential unity of the Venizelist heritage.

I want to suggest here, in accordance with the observations of Hirschon (1989), Stewart (1991), and others, that the division between religious tradition and secular modernity is discursive rather than practical: the former informs the latter in many unexpected ways. Here, then, it is not just the refraction of a quasi-saintly figure such as that of Venizelos through the icon-like properties of stereotypical photographs, nor yet the obvious analogies between the favours granted by saints and Venizelists respectively but also the notion that there is something quintessentially good about political unity. This, of course, is the argument of the state. It is no truer of the state's own *modus operandi*, however, than it is of politicians or of the social life whose kinship and other affective idioms politics exploits so freely.

What we are seeing instead is a situation in which political division is a modern condition, unity an aboriginal legitimation of it. *My* party is always on the side of unity, compromise, probity, virtue. *Yours* is the source of trouble. If, then, by projecting back to a state of unity, we can show that 'we' have 'always' been on the side of good, we can make correspondingly disparaging observations about 'you'. Conversely, if we identify with an obviously losing cause, we may thereby be appealing to a source of unity located outside the immediate conflict. This is neither fatalism nor fecklessness but highly pragmatic realism.

WHO OWNS THE LAND? CHURCH AND PEASANT IN NATIONAL DISCOURSE

In March 1987, the socialist government of Greece announced that it was placing two-thirds of the Orthodox Church's monastic property under the control of agricultural co-operatives. The government's goal was to abolish the class of landless peasants and curry favour with the rural population at large. The measure would also have further undercut the power of the Church, already severely reduced through the introduction of civil marriage under the so-called family laws and threatened by the increasingly vocal pro-socialist clerics within the lower clergy itself.

I do not propose here to give a full account of the conflict. Instead, I shall focus exclusively on its representation in two newspapers published in the small Cretan coastal town of Rethemnos – the pro-government *Rethimno* (hereafter *Re*) and the conservative, pro-opposition *Kritiki Epitheorisi* (hereafter *KE*) – in order to show what elements of historicist *bricolage* came into play. This will clearly show how historical cleavages between right and left produce segmentary readings of history that partly set the local political agenda.

Both parties to the dispute appealed to the basic ideal of unity and accused each other of violating it. In a leading article in the pro-government newspaper entitled 'The Unity of Church and Community Should Be Preserved' (*Re*, 24 March 1987, p. 3), the author – who by announcing himself as 'a politician of the centre' laid unmistakable claim to the Venizelist mantle via George Papandreou's Centre Union party – argued that the real culprits were certain church leaders. The latter, he suggested, espoused the pro-church hierarchical, nationalist, and anti-democratic ideology associated with the 1967 military coup. The writer named several church leaders he considered exempt from the charge, including, first and foremost, Jesus Christ, the Holy Fathers of the Church (i.e., the doctrinal founders), a Cretan bishop 'and other Cretan hierarchs', the Cypriot abbot of a Greek mainland monastery 'where my only daughter is a nun', and a sole abbot on Mount Athos: 'These are the ones of whom I know, without this meaning that there are not hundreds more, humble and worthy ones who constitute the pillars of the Church and the hope of the people and of the Nation [*Ethnos*]'.

The rhetorical strategies used here are very revealing and repay close examination. First of all, there is the obvious attempt to create a 'lineage', starting with Jesus Christ and including all those unnamed 'humble and worthy ones' – these two adjectives being, again, clichés commonly applied in liturgy and sermon alike to Christ. Among the humble, then, are the true bearers of the transcendental unity of Christ. In between come, first of all, the Cretans and the abbot to whose discipline the writer's daughter is subject. Whether this is an attempt to exempt her from disciplinary action as a result of her father's attack on the senior hierarchy of the church is unclear. It is in any case unnecessary for my argument to impute selfish motives to him. The unilineal ideology that informs this list is clear and conceptually independent of the writer's strategic interests. Whatever his personal motives, his support for the governing party entails seeking a lost unity:

> What is above all necessary is the living unity of Church, society, and state, so that they may, together and with the support of all of us, mark out the road to salvation [*sotiria*]. With faith in the god of love [*sto theo tis aghapis*] and with love for humankind and with virtue [*areti*] (simplicity, self-restraint, and moderation), for a new [kind of] just and peaceful human [kind], for a new society of justice and peaceful co-operation, for a new world worthy of living as a *nikokiris* [idealized owner of land] and not as a destroyer of the earth which the Creator gave him.

The soteriological tone is no accident. 'Love' is the condition of the world from which the sin of Adam and Eve drove us and to which we shall return: social redemption and nostalgia for an impossibly unified and loving past (du Boulay 1974: 249; see also Herzfeld 1990) come together with a clearly theological argument designed to persuade the Church hierarchy to give up its land in favour of the humble peasantry just as Jesus abjured wealth in favour of good works. This is the ascetic rhetoric that always marks ecclesiastical populism in Greece, and populism is also an important element of the socialist party's rhetoric.

The newspaper's own reportage, which reflected official thinking, did not differ substantially from the discourse of the invited leader-writer in the respects that concern us here. One staff journalist, for example, argued that the hierarchy's attempt to safeguard the 'substance' (*periousion*) of its holy calling was nothing more than a selfish lien on 'property' (*periousia*) – a telling pun that allowed the pro-government forces to keep their argument within the rhetorical framework of Orthodox doctrine on transubstantiation (*Re*, 9 April 1987, p. 3). At the same time, provoked by the threat emanating from the Patriarchate of Constantinople to revoke the autocephaly of the Orthodox Church of Greece, they also engaged with the larger (i.e., international) political implications of the conflict and brought up a series of issues that have divided the higher clergy from the lower since before the inception of the Greek nation-state.

In particular, the newspaper argued, the Patriarchate had now provoked suspicions of collaboration with the Turkish authorities – a charge that implicitly revived similar accusations relating to the period of the Greek War of Independence. Why, demanded the leader-writer, did the hierarchs not 'raise the banner of Agia Lavra' – a direct allusion to the beginning of the War of Independence in a small Peloponnesian town in 1821 – when the Turks attacked the Greek population of Istanbul or when they invaded Cyprus? 'Can you imagine', thundered the author, 'how [Bishop] Germanos of Old Patras [the leader of the legendary first revolt against the Turks in 1821] would react if he saw you waving the banner of the Revolution of '21 to defend not Freedom and the Independence of the Fatherland but the plots of land, the big buildings, the theatrical businesses, and the discothèques that you exploit?' And he went on to say that in this way all had been revealed, with the 'Revelations, not of [St.] John but of the goals and ambitions of one group of hierarchs'. Again, the evocation of a religious tradition lends authority to an attack against the core of the official Church establishment.

This was a quarrel over transubstantiation of a conceptual kind: religious tradition as the very substance of national identity. A few weeks earlier, the hierarchs had gone on strike, refusing to celebrate the Feast of the Annunciation liturgy on 25 March. This, predictably, had provoked a storm of outrage. It was on 25 March that Bishop Germanos had allegedly led the rebellious forerunners of the revolution to battle. It seemed that the hierarchs were deliberately dissociating themselves from the key *national* event, just as the hierarchy in Constantinople had opposed the revolution in 1821 in a vain attempt to escape the wrath of the Turkish authorities. Another article in *Rethimno* recalled this series of events and commented that the state's action in sequestrating the Church lands was actually the logical final step in disestablishing the Church and so reversing a relationship instituted, in fact, by the Turks.

Such symbolic play on the theme of national enmities also generated discussion about the likely effects of the government's action on the Turks. Conservatives worried that it might not only encourage the Turks to take over the remaining patriarchal properties in Istanbul but also encourage the governments of Israel and Egypt to follow suit (*KE*, 15 March 1987, p. 1). Note the symmetry of discourses here: Just as the pro-government position invoked the rhetoric of Church doctrine, pro-Church advocacy spoke the language of international relations and accused the socialists of committing far greater crimes against the Church than had its most reviled persecutors of yore. Church supporters also (e.g., *KE*, 19 March 1987, p. 1) invoked the mutual identification of Church and people that, at another level, the socialists were also using to deny both the popular base and the religiosity of the senior hierarchs ('Orthodoxy Is Wounded' [*Re*, 21 March 1987, p. 2]).

In the competition over the past as a scarce resource, both sides necessarily respect a set of common rules which constitute the enabling grounds of the dispute (Appadurai 1981). We should add, however, that the specific content of the rules may also change as a consequence of the victory of one side or another. In the largely anti-clerical island of Crete, the conservatives' use of populist language built on an existing tradition of rhetorical borrowing.

The arguments about the Church lands do not dispute certain 'essential' truths: the significance of the Church and of the Christian religion in Greek history and identity, the importance of humility and poverty, the moral exclusion of Jews and Muslims, and the moral validity of unity. Instead, they refract these principles through the factional divisions of modern political life. The Greek-Turkish opposition becomes a manipulable symbolic device whereby each side organizes its own ideas about the present. Time, as Thompson argues, is 'telescoped' – not, however, in the sense of some structural amnesia that simply leaves out intervening generations but through a principle of identification between seemingly similar events, where similarity is itself constructed according to the cut of one's ideological cloth.

Thus, the socialists liken the hierarchs to the Turks by simple association. The conservatives, instead, argue that it is the socialist government that should be considered heir to the Turkish persecutors and to all other infidels besides. Similar manipulations beset the theme of unity. The socialists call on the hierarchs to stop breaking the essential unity of the Church, validated by the grounding of the lower clergy (and perhaps some privileged local bishops as well) in the industrial labourer and peasant classes. The conservatives, by contrast, locate that unity in an unshakable mutuality of interest binding Church, state, and people and treat the government in Athens as the betrayer of this harmonious ideal. Both appeal to the lost condition of *aghapi* (love), a theological construct that also underlies social notions of *anthropia* (common humanity), itself invoked by both sides in defence of their respective positions.

What are the key figures in these competing accounts of the present conflict? First of all, all present attitudes are based on readings of the past. For those who support the Church, the arguments are all based on the alleged unity of Church and people and the role of the Church in battling *against* the Turks. The other side splits the hierarchs away from the popularly based clergy and accuses the hierarchs of being, in effect, *pro-Turkish* – the same symbolic device whereby Capodistrias called the landed primates of mainland Greece 'Turkish Greeks' at the time of the Revolution and whereby opponents of the conservative government in Athens at the time of the 1981 elections that brought the socialists to power hinted that the former were really Turks, too (e.g., 'they've been in power for 400 years', a common cliché for the Tourkokratia [Herzfeld 1985: 19]).

Another concern is that the conservatives, with their more

pro-Western sympathies, were especially anxious not to reveal a split in the national church, whereas the government – precisely in order to show that the hierarchs were *not* good nationalists – attempted to present this not as an internal split but as an act of exclusion. Certainly socialists are no more willing to wash what *they* regard as dirty linen in public. A passionate socialist supporter, for example, was especially indignant when he read in the paper that Mitsotakis had accused Papandreou of selling out national interests at Davos; in his opinion such statements exposed Greek internal divisions to international publicity. But this gives us some insight into the meaning of 'betrayal' in Greek political rhetoric.

One can only betray those who are defined as 'one's own'. Thus, from a populist and anti-clerical perspective, it was the hierarchy (not the ecclesiastical rank and file) that betrayed the nation by taking what was seen as a pro-Turkish position; in this view the hierarchs constituted the ethical fifth column, *as they had done in the past*. For the conservatives, by contrast, the hierarchs had always paid for their noble commitment to the Greek cause, even the cautious Patriarch of Constantinople at the time of the Greek War of Independence having paid for his coreligionists' rebelliousness with his life. Today, therefore, the actions of the government continued as internal betrayal committed a national crime that, as one article put it, had never been perpetrated even in the darkest days of persecution.

ELECTORAL LEMMINGS OR SOCIAL SQUIRRELS?

The concept of 'betrayal' is a common theme in Greek popular historiography. Folksongs that describe the sack of citadels in the days of the Turkish invasion often attribute the ultimate success of the invaders to the existence of a single rotten apple – the Greek who is not truly a Greek. Nowadays, too, in ordinary social interaction, the concept is often employed to explain how the authorities – the Turks of social life, as it were – manage to penetrate one's secrets: jealous neighbours, rival business interests, even disaffected kin.

This brings me to a central theme: the importance of identifying the figurative devices that key all historical discourse (see White 1978) and that help us to find the common ground of official historiography, day-by-day journalism, and local gossip.

The traitor within is certainly one such figure. Arguments about *who* the traitor is – the church? the government? – show that all sides to these disputes share a body of figurative models that make dispute possible. Indeed, one could say that arguments about the present draw on models of the past in which contenders simply assign different conventional roles to different actors, according to their respective predilections.

Against the traitor we must set the heroic figure of the political actor who refuses to desert the cause even when all seems lost. Such apparently quixotic loyalty conflicts with other models of Greek identity, and in many situations it looks silly and nothing else. On the whole, one gets little admiration for sticking to one's guns when it is clear that all is lost. And yet there is also a considerable risk in deserting the sinking ship. The question is then with what *identity* one wishes to be labelled.

In some cases, of course, there is not much choice. In local elections in the mountain village I have called Glendi, when one patrigroup had to 'go it alone' without benefit of client patrigroups (they had all become disgusted with its internecine struggles and the emergence of a weak leader), not only did virtually all patrigroup members vote for the doomed slate but also they provided all its candidate slots. In that way, the reputation of the patrigroup survived the ultimate humiliation: no internal fissures were placed on view, and indeed, by a sort of sociological sleight-of-hand, the existing fissures (subsegment divisions) were presented as transcendent unity (the slate) (see Herzfeld 1985: 100–6). In a less extreme and much commoner scenario, some candidates agree to stand knowing that even if their slate wins they themselves will not get a seat because they have simply been put in as a makeweight. Again, there are some rewards for being able to say that one supported the slate even if one's personal fortune was threatened. Such politicians simply merge their identities with the larger good – a common figure in Greek political discourse.

What kinds of calculation are likely to have motivated those who supported the third-party candidate? Siding with the winners can gain one material advantages but can also damage one's social standing, especially if it is thought that one has 'betrayed one's own' for immediate personal gain. Siding with the losers, superficially a quixotic gesture, at least keeps the polluting figure of the traitor at bay. The idiom of kinship reinforces this pattern of discrimination. One socialist described a conservative candidate both as 'lacking a patriline [of his own]' and as an *anemazoksaris*, that is, one who has 'married in' to a virilocal community – even though Rethemnos is increasingly uxorilocal! – and said that the 'genuine' (*ghnisii*, a term possibly implying blood connections) right-wingers probably would not vote for him because they had 'their own'.

In the 1986 municipal elections in Rethemnos, it was very clear that either the socialist Khristos Skouloudis or the conservative Dimitris Arkhondakis would win. The independent left-winger, Babis Pramateftakis, did not stand a chance. It is clear why supporters of the two main candidates kept proclaiming imminent victory: these pronouncements were performative utterances whose felicity would be tested in the ballot-box. An ambitious younger person might stand on such a slate even when the chances of winning a seat were small. One of the socialists told me that he did it to support the party (the theme of hero vs. traitors) and that he did not want to be seen as part of the mayor's clique ('if I want, my voice will be heard louder than the mayor's' – because he was also head of the association of heads of large families, a powerful organization on Crete). What looked initially like a very atypical mode, opting out of the political limelight, thus turned out to be bravado. This man knew that he would not get elected but that he might expect some benefits later and that he also maintained his local standing by appearing as a concerned citizen who would not lord it over his neighbours. His own predictable defeat could be enfolded in the scenario of 'his' party's victory, a victory to which he contributed as a makeweight without sacrificing personal autonomy or diminishing his local political base.

After a run-off election, his leader was indeed elected mayor. Since he had also said that 'the mayor is not made by his personality, it's the councillors who make him', he had cleverly managed to anticipate the increasing disaffection generated by Skouloudis's often impatient mien and thus dissociate himself from the long-term failure of the temporarily victorious slate or from Skouloudis's eventual desertion of the socialist party.

What, then, of those who supported third-party candidate Pramateftakis? Here the social calculus has, if anything, a still greater role to play. The historical figure of the traitor is not one with which most left-wingers want to be associated. Shunned by even the moderate centre and the right, they have suffered greatly in the civil war from persecution largely instigated by police informers, very often drawn from their own circle of kin and friends. They describe their solidarity in a language drawn directly from the idiom of kinship. Thus, once a person has declared leftist allegiances, it takes unusual courage or insouciance to abandon the cause.

It is in this context, I suggest, that grand declarations about an impending victory that no one realistically expects must be understood. Electoral upsets do, of course, occur. But the point would seem to be, rather, that people previously involved in union activity or conflict with the authorities have relatively little to gain amongst their peers by supporting either of the two main parties. They may instead advance their reputation for high principles by fighting for a lost cause whose ultimate defeat will justify their most darkly muttered fears of persecution of the working classes by a graft-ridden and wicked conservative political establishment. In a democratic era when all the communist parties have legal status, it is hard to claim such persecution unless one has first tried to establish the rhetorical *possibility* of victory. That done, and the inevitable defeat having occurred instead, each party supporter can represent his or her own fight as reasonable and the current distress as the product of superior forces and of trickery. The state, always under the control of the major parties, must be a 'thief' because so are those parties. The figurative exegesis passes muster simply because it fits existing conventions about betrayal, theft, and persecution.

Such conventions permit a justification of present actions in terms of a particular reading of the past, a narrative plot on which all actors agree *structurally* (Appadurai's 'rules') even though they disagree radically about its *realization in specific events*. People 'make history' by assimilating themselves and those they claim as 'theirs' to particular 'mythemes' in this plot. Paradoxically, the successful use of a rhetoric of humility and principle may be the best proof one can offer of self-regard, while the anticipation of disaster shows that actors may and do plan future action with a variety of goals in mind. Self-regard, like such other stereotypes as 'amoral familism' (Banfield 1958) and the 'image of limited good' (Foster 1965), is in Greece less a reality of modern small-town politics than a rhetorical strategy directed against one's opponents. In some situations, suppressing self-regard may be more profitable than too obviously adopting it. If one wishes to desert a winning cause or champion a losing one, this must be done as an act of devil-may-care braggadocio that others will certainly try to decry as stupidity. If one wishes to champion a winning cause or desert a losing one, one may be able to justify this as common sense, but one's detractors can always adumbrate it to the narrative plot of the traitor within. Thus, self-interest is not *automatically* served by doing the things that self-interest would most obviously seem to recommend. History provides the means of creating opposite interpretations, and these in turn affect one's own place in the history of the local community, a refraction – in an ultimately segmentary world – of the larger historical entity, the nation.

CONCLUDING REMARKS: 'THE MEEK SHALL INHERIT THE EARTH'

The rhetorical space in which modern Greeks conduct their political struggles has already been mapped out by a Christian ideology to which, at many levels, they are practically opposed. Meekness and *eghoismos* hardly go together; there is a strong anti-ecclesiastical tradition in Crete especially, and the calculus of intention and feasibility that to some extent governs actors' decisions and actions is in conflict with the ostensible logic of mutual love, co-operation, and respect that it nevertheless mines to great effect. We owe to John Campbell (1964) the important insight that Christian religious rhetoric may furnish the means of adjusting doctrine to the exigencies of social life.

This is not a question of belief, which is a problematical category at best, but one of collective representations and the uses to which actors can put them. Among these representations are images of the past, images that guide orientations to future action. If a communist who has backed the losing faction seems to follow in a soteriological tradition, this is not only because he can ill afford to reject the Christianity which is such an important part of his claim to participatory rights in the Greek polity but because the associated idiom is the only one that Greeks at all points on the political continuum can be reasonably sure of sharing. As I have argued elsewhere (Herzfeld 1990), soteriological and eschatological language may allow social actors to adapt the idea of a perfectly ordered past, or structural nostalgia, to the harsh experiences of a fractious present.

Folklorists of nationalist persuasion draw a hard-and-fast line between history and folklore. It should now be clearer why they must. The division is based on a premise of absolute facticity, history being the objective stream from which folklore creatively drinks. Even 'historical songs' are seen as fictional elaborations or simplifications of fact. And here is the crux of the matter: simplicity is a statistical criterion, set by a discursive operator as a baseline for the determination of what constitutes fact and what does not. It is an important constituent of structural nostalgia, because it is what renders structure transparent and therefore describable. Once we watch the same figures in play in social life, whether through newspaper reportage or in the rough-and-tumble of local electoral politics (to take the two scenarios used here), we realize that the writing of history participates in the same processes of factual determination as these seemingly more ephemeral interactions. The narrative plots that folklorists have developed are in fact so closely tied to those enacted by social actors engaged in current political struggles that separating them out prevents us from fully appreciating why such rhetorical strategies appear to work.

And why *do* they work? I submit that it is through their conventionality that – along with excuses, for example (see Austin 1971) – they make, if not plausible, then certainly acceptable the outrageous claims of social actors who thereby further their pursuit of strategic interests, converting rhetorical advantage into social and material gains. It is here that we have to be especially careful to note that the supposed pursuit of self-interest in local societies – contrary to the stereotypical models – is in fact precisely the practical embodiment of that collective selfhood that lies at the basis of virtually all ideologies of modern European statism.

NOTE

1 The field research on which this article is based was conducted during tenure of a Fellowship for Independent Study and Research from the National Endowment for the Humanities (U.S.A.) in 1986–7. I am greatly indebted to the Endowment for this support. I would also like to express my warm gratitude to Kirsten Hastrup for the invitation to participate in her panel at the Coimbra conference and for her

helpful editorial suggestions on my paper. Responsibility for the paper itself is of course entirely my own. I have used the form Rethemnos (rather than Rethimno) in deference to local usage.

REFERENCES

Anderson, Benedict (1983) *Imagined Communities: Reflections on the Origin and Spread of Nationalism*, London: Verso.

Appadurai, Arjun (1981) 'The past as a scarce resource', *Man*, n.s., 16: 201–19.

Austin, J. L. (1971 [1956–7]) 'A plea for excuses', in Colin Lyas (ed.) *Philosophy and Linguistics*, London: Macmillan.

Banfield, Edward C. (1958) *The Moral Basis of a Backward Society*, Glencoe: Free Press.

Bourdieu, Pierre (1977) *Outline of a Theory of Practice*, trans. Richard Nice, Cambridge: Cambridge University Press.

Campbell, J. K. (1964) *Honour, Family, and Patronage: A Study of Institutions and Moral Values in a Greek Mountain Community*, Oxford: Clarendon Press.

Dresch, Paul (1986) 'The significance of the course events take in segmentary systems', *American Ethnologist* 13: 309–24.

du Boulay, Juliet (1974) *Portrait of a Greek Mountain Village*, Oxford: Clarendon Press.

Evans-Pritchard, E. E. (1956) *The Nuer Religion*, Oxford: Clarendon Press.

Fernandez, James W. (1974) 'The mission of metaphor in expressive culture', *Current Anthropology* 15: 119–45.

Foster, George (1965) 'Peasant society and the image of limited good', *American Anthropologist* 67: 293–315.

Geertz, Clifford (1973) *The Interpretation of Cultures*, New York: Basic Books.

Handler, Richard (1988) *Nationalism and the Politics of Culture in Quebec*, Madison: University of Wisconsin Press.

Herzfeld, Michael (1985) *The Poetics of Manhood: Contest and Identity in a Cretan Mountain Village*, Princeton: Princeton University Press.

—— (1987) *Anthropology through the Looking-Glass: Critical Ethnography in the Margins of Europe*, Cambridge: Cambridge University Press.

—— (1990) 'Pride and perjury: time and the oath in the mountain villages of Crete', *Man*, n.s., 25: 305–22.

—— (1991) *A Place in History: Social and Monumental Time in a Cretan Town*, Princeton: Princeton University Press.

Hirschon, Renée (1989) *Heirs to the Greek Catastrophe*, Oxford: Clarendon Press.

Karp, Ivan, and Maynard, Kent (1983) 'Reading *The Nuer*', *Current Anthropology* 21: 481–503.

Meeker, Michael E. (1979) *Literature and Violence in North Arabia*, Cambridge: Cambridge University Press.

Stewart, Charles (1985) '*Exotika*: Greek values and their supernatural antitheses', *Scandinavian Yearbook of Folklore* 41: 37–64.
—— (1991) *Demons and the Devil: Moral Imagination in Modern Greek Culture*, Princeton: Princeton University Press.
Thompson, Michael (1979) *Rubbish Theory: The Creation and Destruction of Value*, Oxford: Oxford University Press.
White, Hayden (1978) *Tropics of Discourse: Essays in Cultural Criticism*, Baltimore: Johns Hopkins University Press.

Chapter 5

Dual histories
A Mediterranean problem

Anne Knudsen

'History' may mean different things. It may refer to a society's self-representation in written or told stories about the past or to concrete social circumstances, actions, and developments. Different stories about the past can be seen as representing different modes for the society which produces them.

Much of European philosophical and theoretical historical debate[1] during the 1980s turned around the relation between history as a (self-)representational *genre* and the specificity of societies which believe themselves to be moving through time, developing and expanding, 'maturing' and 'living', as it were. The general notion structuring this debate is that it is only modernity in post-revolutionary Europe and the U.S.A. that has fostered the concept of history as an objective condition of this semi-biological and narratively well-defined sort. The thesis is that only state-organized, imperialistically expanding, rapidly changing, and economically successful modern society gives rise to progressive history as a mode of thinking and hence of self-representation. History as a *genre* and history as a specific mode for society are therefore viewed as two sides of the same coin. A corollary to this thesis is that only within modernity would a narrated history of the modern kind be regarded as a representation of objectively existing chains of events and therefore present conditions as the result of a logical or necessary development.

In the following I shall outline a problem of history as a question of political events and structural changes within a specific society. I shall discuss the social and cultural conditions for a change from one kind of history to another and thus address the problem of distinguishing between a traditional society and a society on the path of historical development.

LOOKING BACK ON MODERNITY

The image of peasant culture was an intrinsic part of the nine-teenth-century articulation of European progress, urbanization, and national homogenization. As is apparent in countless museums of peasant culture,[2] peasants were viewed as living not in the realm of progressive history characteristic of the nine-teenth-century economic and political self-image of *la mission civilisatrice* but in a sort of non-time – a cyclical, sleepy, tra-ditional life in which wars and seasons were met with an equally patient lack of protest or understanding. Peasant culture was viewed as stable, unchanging, timeless; the only notion of *time* found in connection with the definition of peasant culture was the *point* in time marking its demise or its awakening to political or religious consciousness.

This image has been increasingly criticized with regard to its applicability to the extra-European societies of classical anthro-pological research. On the one hand, it has been rather convin-cingly demonstrated that the societies of Sub-Saharan Africa and South America at the moment of 'contact' were not the stable, primitive societies imagined by European travellers but rather the results of a social collapse following demographic catas-trophes caused by European diseases (see, e.g., Thornton 1983; Friedman 1983; Petersen 1987–8). The diseases travelled inland before the Europeans with an estimated two-year lead, killing huge percentages of the population. In East Africa, European cattle diseases had all but exterminated the herds of the interior well before any European set eyes on the herdsmen. On the other hand, it has been argued that independent historical devel-opments had in fact taken place in the societies which seemed 'stable' to their European colonizers, who then proceeded to change them to conform to the image of stability. British coloni-zation can, for example, be argued to have brought about struc-tural changes in India by solidifying a fluctuating and highly negotiable caste concept into a rigid, unchanging system (see Pedersen 1985). Likewise, the indirect rule of what were under-stood as African tribes can be seen as the preservation of a momentary state of affairs as a timeless primitive order.

Both kinds of critique suggest that the pre-contact societies were possibly just as 'history-producing' as contemporary Euro-pean ones. But while it is evident that the image of 'primitive society' formed a useful counter-image to the European self-understanding of progressive civilization,[3] it is much less evident that all societies are equally prone to change – to 'producing history'. Just as one cannot without argument presume that 'different' societies have not changed since the dawn of time, one cannot presume that the one thing common to all societies is their propensity to change.

One way of approaching this question is to do historical research with the question in mind. Another way is to ask how it has become possible to put it at all. The metaphor 'the past is a foreign country' has not always been current in European thought. This idea and many others about culture, ethnicity, etc., can be seen as signs that something has changed in the European self-image. The completely natural and self-evident understanding of modern European patterns of behaviour, moral values, options, and aspirations as identical with the universal, truly historical meaning of all human life on the planet has given way to a much less self-sufficient attitude of doubt, fear of the future, and scepticism as regards *les grandes histoires*, be they economic or political, socialist or liberalist evolutionary. In my opinion the European critique of *les grandes histoires* is related not only to the impending nuclear ending of them which has worried philosophers such as Bernard-Henri Lévy and André Glucksmann but also to the more general lack of power and influence experienced by the post-colonial European states in the era of super-powers. Thus, while it now seems somewhat less probable than during the eighties that history will end with the opening of the missile silos, the end of European political and economic supremacy has brought an end to the speed-blindness which has prevented us from seeing the landscapes of the past.[4]

Modernity's image of the past is the construction of progressive, expanding, history-producing centres surrounded by a traditionalist, unchanging, culture-produced periphery, whether extra-European or merely 'peasant'. In this image the stability of traditional society poses no theoretical problems; it is merely the logical – indeed, necessary – counterpart to the changing modern aspects of world society. Traditional customs are seen as remaining unaltered until something or someone alters them – until 'modernization', fragmentation, or the like sets in. The moment modernity's self-assurance falters, however, both parts of this image are shattered. The kind of social change called 'history' and the kind of social stability called 'traditional society' simultaneously become theoretical problems. Whereas social change has hitherto been regarded as a kind of side-effect to history – which has seemed an objective condition – and traditional society as a society not yet touched by history, the causes for history must now be sought in specific forms of social organization.

In this situation, the anthropological[5] notion of 'society' as a generalized category comprising fast-changing, slow-changing, and unchanging societies seems to provide a useful framework for analysis. One of the new questions put by historical anthropology is therefore how historical change comes about at all. This represents a challenge to anthropology not least because historians today seem increasingly inclined to put aside this question in favour of a vision of the past as composed of cultural islands, as it were, each with its own stable social forms.[6]

THE WESTERN MEDITERRANEAN: A DUAL HISTORY

The lands surrounding the Western Mediterranean basin have been the theatre of some of the most impressive empires in history. They have also been the arena of countless uprisings against central powers of whatever kind. While each particular uprising throughout the centuries in, for example, today's Algeria or in Corsica can of course be explained with reference to specific conditions of its time, what cannot as easily be understood is the *similarity* of the values professed by uprisings centuries apart. In central North Africa as well as in Corsica, uprisings are so uniform in their ideology as to amount to a single one reviving over and over again. Roughly speaking, all these movements are politically egalitarian and socially ascetic; they are turned against central powers as such. Within the historical record not one century has been without its uprising in either area. To complicate the question further, this phenomenon cannot be viewed as the confrontation of a uniform 'local' dislike of power with an 'external' state-building culture. Several of the uprisings have ended in the formation of central governments no less hierarchical than the ones they had opposed (see Julien 1931).

What we are confronted with in this area seems to be not only a dual history but a kind of dual society. By this I mean that these societies remain 'traditional' in the sense that they seem to have rather stable egalitarian social values but also produce 'history' in the sense that they create social hierarchies, military expansion, expanding power structures, and even some degree of technical and economic innovation. Not only the one or the other thus needs explanation and theoretical understanding: the combination of the two represents a particular challenge to historical anthropology. This apparent contradiction can be studied in detail for specific periods of time in specific areas. Here I will outline the events of the mid-eighteenth century in Corsica.

JUSTICE AND RULERS

The first democratic constitution in modern Europe was adopted in the central Corsican city of Corti in mid-November 1755[7] by the General Assembly of the Corsican republic (see Carrington 1974). The independent nation of Corsica was a constitutional democracy with universal (male) suffrage for fourteen years before losing its independence to a French army nearly equalling the island's male population in numbers (see, e.g., Pomponi 1971; 1978; 1979; 1981). The uprising leading to the constitution of Corti was only the latest in a century-long series of rebellions, several of which had explicit democratic claims.

During the mediaeval period the island of Corsica was handed down from one Italian city-state to another as a former possession of the Roman empire. A particularly violent uprising in the early decades of the fourteenth century put an end to Pisan rule and abolished feudalism in the island in favour of a village democracy *a popolo e commune*. Feudalism was never re-established in the northern part of the island. All descriptions from the eighteenth century onward note that differences in wealth are insignificant in Corsica: there are no landless and no large estates.

Longest and last the island was ruled by Genoa, the senate of which took over the rule from the Genoese Banco San Giorgio in 1571 after another violent uprising. By the early eighteenth century the statutes of 1571 were still in force though obsolete even by the European standards of the day. What struck outside observers such as Montesquieu or Voltaire as particularly unreasonable was Genoese law enforcement, a jurisdiction entirely dependent on the personal whims of the year's governor. An accused had no rights whatsoever, not even the right of having a verdict made known to him before he was sent off to the galleys.

The first serious uprising of the eighteenth century was, however, prompted by hunger. In the winter of 1729–30 the Genoese tax collectors totally overlooked the fact that the year's harvest had been a disaster. The peasants of the interior rose and killed the tax collectors and their armed escorts before marching on to the administrative centres on the coast, several of which were sacked during the Christmas holidays. The Genoese reprisals were harsh and indiscriminate. During the spring of 1730, whole villages were burnt down and supposed ringleaders publicly executed in cruel and spectacular fashions. This proved no deterrent. The whole northern part of the island rose in rage, electing leaders who were not the starving poor but educated men of some local standing. According to contemporary sources (Rostini 1881–2), the hunger revolt had turned into a 'revolution'. For the following thirty-nine years, the only periods of comparative peace in the island were associated with the intervention of foreign armies such as the Austrians and the French (see, e.g., Jaussin 1758; Officier du régiment 1889). Both these powers at different times negotiated with the Corsican rebels on behalf of Genoa and reported to their Genoese allies that the rebellion could not be quelled by armed intervention. Several of the generals involved actually wrote letters to the effect that the Genoese had only themselves to blame for their troubles in Corsica (Varnhagen von Ense 1894).

Meanwhile, the Corsican leaders deftly took advantage of their access to the European public (Boswell 1768) through contacts with foreign officers and diplomats (Marchini 1983), pamphlets (Arrighi and Castellin 1983), open letters to the European rulers, and private correspondence with influential persons (Arrighi and Castellin 1980). Many of the Corsican leaders had been exiled for political crimes, and an impressive number of them had university educations from Italian universities, notably Pisa and Naples. The works of Montesquieu were among the possessions of at least one of the leaders (Paoli 1885 [1754]) and Rousseau and James Boswell among his correspondents. A central theme in all the Corsican statements was the question of justice. All pointed to the frequency of manslaughter as the worst of all Corsican problems, and all placed the responsibility for this state of affairs with the arbitrary Genoese law enforcement. Several texts claim that up to 900 men were killed in vendettas each year in Corsica (Arrighi and Castellin 1983: 15), where the total population at the time is estimated at 175,000 souls.

This preoccupation with justice is not just a question of rhetoric. The actual text of the constitution mirrors the problem. Only one-quarter of the text concerns political institutions; the rest is devoted to criminal law and a detailed structure of courts of justice. Most striking, it is around questions of justice that the constitution differs most from its evident Montesquieu inspiration. The General Assembly – which according to the text is in sole possession of legitimate supremacy on the island – elected the same person *capo generale* (head of state), supreme military commander, and judge of the supreme court. Since the army was also functioning as police force and the court had the right to prosecute for the public, the *capo generale* thus combined in his person all of society's powers, in flagrant contradiction of the contemporary political philosophy which had furnished the overall concept for the constitution.

FROM EQUALITY TO POWER

To understand a democratic revolution which proceeds to elect autocratic leaders and develop dictatorial structures of government, questions of justice need to be closely examined. Not only did the independent Corsican nation seem to be obsessed with the idea of justice; the importance of law enforcement was evident for more than a century after its fall.[8]

All sources agree that vendettas were responsible for the majority of murders on the island during the eighteenth century. This would seem confirmed by the fact that almost all the murders committed during the first half of the nineteenth century can be demonstrated to belong in this context (Knudsen 1989). During the first half of the century, the murders recorded annually by French forces of order ranged from 82 (1826) to 239 (1849), with an average of just over 138.[9] The explanations given in contemporary sources for this disturbing state of affairs are of two kinds. One is first set forth in the pamphlet *Disinganno intorno alla guerra di Corsica*[10] and repeated by many writers: that the lack or malfunction of formal justice compels – or even encourages – Corsicans to take justice into their own hands, taking vengeance for crimes that ought to have been punished by the courts of justice. The other is explicitly contradicted by Natali (Arrighi and Castellin 1983: 23), which suggests that it was already current in his time; it was the explanation that was the favourite of nineteenth-century romantic travellers, poets, novelists, and the general public (Mérimée 1964 [1840]: 40; Robiquet 1835: 393) – that Corsicans are more passionate than other people and that the 'passion de la vengeance' is dominant in 'le génie des corses'. As can be seen, the first explanation is dependent on the second (Wilson 1989); not all populations living without efficient law enforcement kill each other in such numbers. The preoccupation of the Corsican government with justice seems to reveal a trait specific to Corsican society.

STRUCTURAL INDETERMINATION

The apparent contradiction found in the independent Corsican nation between a constitution establishing democracy as an ideal and a political practice in which the head of state had absolute power was paralleled in the practice of the island's population. On the one hand, liberty, equality, and justice were universally recognized values in island society; on the other, Corsicans accepted no justice other than that which each exacted himself, a justice which seemed to his enemies (including Corsicans) unjust and outrageous.

In Corsica, as in many 'traditional' European societies, we find an instability linked to the very reproduction of society's basic groups. While Corsican society constantly and uniformly referred to the family as the foundation of society, it lacked the most elementary precondition for the clear establishment of concrete families: an unambiguous kinship system. Countless references to 'family values' run through all the sources on Corsican society, but the definition of this 'family' is very ambiguous. All the texts pretend that the definition of the family is obvious, to the point that it is difficult to find a description of the Corsican kinship system. But if family, kin group, or the like is to be the elementary group in society, it must be unambiguously defined *in practice*.

The *Statuti civili e criminali di Corsica* (Gregorj 1843; cf. Fontana 1905) were established in 1571 and remained in force in 1755. They are quite clear as regards ownership rights: only individuals can own lands, flocks, houses, or the like. In such a system, inheritance indicates the extent and character of notions of kinship, material goods being almost a metaphor for 'blood'. The chapters in the *Statuti* dealing with inheritance reveal a kinship system which is patrilineal overall but has some bilineal traits. Notably, the relationship between maternal grandfather and grandson contradicts the patrilineality of the system: this grandchild in fact inherits from his maternal grandfather. Thus, while women do not inherit from either their fathers or their brothers (or their husbands, for that matter) but are only given a dowry of the same value as a male's share of the inheritance, their sons belong not only to their fathers' lineages but also to their mothers'. The structural consequences of this anomaly are apparent.

Since every man has a mother and therefore a consanguineal link to his mother's father, it is impossible to create distinct family or kinship groups. No kinship-defined group has clear limits, everyone being tendentially a member of several such groups. The society can thus not be 'composed of families', since these families are fictions rather than verifiable, genealogically produced facts. In order to create *actual* groups, kinship principles must be supplemented by other principles which make it possible to establish a hierarchy of 'blood ties' and thus to neglect some of them in favour of others.

KINSHIP STRATEGIES

Many of the traits which puzzled observers of Corsican society in the late eighteenth century can be understood as strategies to this end. Endogamy (Ravis-Giordani 1983: 359ff.) served as a means of limiting the range of relatives admitted into the kinship network, but this strategy had its disadvantages. Notably, the internal organization of, for instance, a village composed of a single kin group still posed the problem of hierarchization, since no 'centre' of the structure could be found where everyone had several different kinship relations with everyone else. When disagreements came up in such a village – over grazing rights, water, flocks, or any of every day's trivia – the number of 'traitors' (Knudsen 1985: 65–87) named by the participants bears witness to the difficulties of such a lack of structuring principles; everyone claimed the support of everyone else on the ground of 'family loyalty'. The strategy of endogamy sometimes even worsened the initial problem – that of determining the exact relation between each individual and any other *in terms of kinship*.

To aggravate the situation, the specific Corsican variety of the dowry system ran counter to any effort to subordinate maternal kinship ties *vis-à-vis* paternal ones. The dowry system resulted in a sort of 'double unilineality', where not only were dowries passed on in a maternal blood line but the dowry remained the legitimate possession of the woman in question and could never form part of her husband's possessions. Since women were always legally dependent on men, the male relatives of any woman kept land rights in the affinal family. Finally, the dowry could be inherited only by direct descendants of the woman who had originally brought it: if her line died out, the dowry went back to her lineage, no matter how long ago the marriage transaction had taken place.[11] Maternal links could not be ignored or neglected.

The obvious response to these complications was the same as one finds in many Mediterranean societies with similar structural problems; society's members referred not only to kinship but to a wide range of other parameters in order to establish actual groups. There were kinship ties that counted and others that did not. But such a system of distinctions does not work automatically. *Clanisme* (Pomponi 1978) in Corsica consists in the combination of a *kinship ideology*[12] with a reality which might rightly be labelled 'political', a reality of personalized and reciprocal links, of relationships of choice, dependency, and influence: *power relations*. It is only with the establishment of a hierarchy *among individuals* that it becomes possible to distinguish between 'relatives' in terms of their importance.

However, a social system of this kind – a personalized, political system – has its own effects and creates its own problems. One of the effects is the importance such a system attaches to the individual man, be he a 'clan member' or a political leader.

A PEOPLE OF KINGS

In daily practice, the ideology of kinship could not serve as a guide for group formation. In order to organize real groups that could be distinguished from their surroundings and from other groups, there had to be a personalized centre. Groups were composed around an individual man in relation to whom a group of relatives could be counted and counted upon.

Two kinds of behaviour seem to have served this purpose. One was to be a 'politician', which in this context was equivalent to having a certain talent for organization, a certain number of dependent supporters, and an acute sense of diplomacy and political strategy. Anyone who could attract a number of adherents, satisfy their demands, and thwart the ambitions of their adversaries was on his way to becoming a *capo*. What rendered this career difficult was the men already in power – and the ambition of every other man. The other way of becoming the centre of a group of recognized relatives was to kill or be killed. Naturally, this cannot really be understood as a 'political strategy', but it is evident that whenever a relative was killed or became a murderer a kin group would form around him with a view to the ensuing vendetta. One can indeed argue that the vendetta groupings were the *only* clearly defined kinship groups in eighteenth- and nineteenth-century Corsica, notably because involvement in a vendetta rendered one's affiliation to one group or another irrevocable.[13]

These two ways of creating kinship groups were equally dependent on a central individual. The Corsican notion of honour can be understood as the socially recognized aspect of the importance attached to the individual in this society which professed collectivistic ideas but practised an extreme form of individualism, practically all important decisions being made at the level of the individual (man).[14]

To create a level of power transcending local structures – a nation – the Corsicans seem to have proceeded in much the same way as they did locally. A large part of the process of creating the independent Corsican nation consisted in political struggles between *grands hommes*, locally powerful men. But the greatest impediment to the formation of a single structure for political competition – and thus for a transcendent notion of 'society' – was the competing structuring principle of private vengeance, private justice, and private war. Questions of justice and vengeance provided by far the most frequent occasion for the creation of competing structures, corporate groups of a non-governmental or even anti-governmental kind, and it is therefore logical that a constitution trying to assemble Corsicans in one socio-political structure should have focused on questions of justice.

TRANSCENDENT VALUES: JUSTICE AND NATION

The idea of justice was inherent in the structure of the vendetta. Murders were committed in the name of justice, and murderers viewed themselves as enforcers of justice. Thus it would be obvious in practical terms not only that all governmental efficiency depended on the monopolization of justice[15] but also that governmental legitimacy was closely linked to the notion of justice. Anyone who could present himself as the embodiment of justice would occupy a strongly invested position in Corsican society. But this position was not easy to obtain, first of all because every man claimed it as his own – and who could tell whether he was right? In this domain, too, the only proof would be the practice – the fact of doing justice. To do justice in the name of society (and not only in the name of family honour, thus simply taking vengeance) one would have to be in a power position already; this would be the only way of avoiding the vengeance of the victims of one's verdicts. Just as the practice of private vengeance tended to produce an increasingly fragmented society, with ever-increasing numbers of private judges, a power position invested with an actual and impartial judicial practice reinforced itself: to practise justice was to enhance one's power position, which reinforced the efficiency of justice, which reinforced the power position, and so on.

Thus it seems that the very confusion in independent Corsica of the 'powers' of society separated by Montesquieu was the means that brought this society into 'history', or even 'modernity'. To assemble the inhabitants of the island in one social structure – Corsica – fundamental changes had to take place. Though Corsican society was already oriented towards individualism, social equality, and justice, the practising of these values constituted a social system in which no single focus for power could hold out for long. The vendetta provided one way of organizing groups and political alliance another. Only by combining the two could an integrated system be developed.

It is logical that the *capo generale* should have figured in both systems, as an elected political leader and as head of justice. Only by embodying the total society's impersonal justice could the head of state escape from the competition of his many equals – and only as the supreme military commander and thus in possession of armed forces could the high judge escape from the competition of other, private judges and their competing justice. The equality of Corsican men can therefore be seen as the very condition for absolute power, the concentration in the hands of one man of several structural positions. And since the ideology of equality persisted, there is no reason the Corsican democracy could not have developed a modernizing state with the characteristic ever-increasing distance between ordinary – equal – men and the institutions of power, justice, and society-in-general, a state on the path of history.

During the last months of its existence, the independent Corsican republic in many ways anticipated developments which would later characterize the First French Republic.[16] The political negotiations between Paoli and Choiseul were rendered difficult by the increasing unity and nationalism of the General Assembly, which laid aside internal differences in the name of the common cause (Hall 1971; Arrighi 1966). In the same way the total mobilization of the male population against the French army in 1768 can be seen as an indication that the Corsican attitude was no longer dominated by the family perspective. Versailles was greatly surprised by the amplitude of Corsican resistance, and the historian might well be, too. Whereas during earlier campaigns there had been no lack of Corsicans who would collaborate with the enemy of their next-door neighbour, the struggle of 1768–9 involved almost every village in the island on the Corsican side. This was actually a 'young nation'[17] united in defence of its independence, a fact which is demonstrated not only by the repeated reinforcements of the French army necessary to subdue the island but also by the extraordinary drop in numbers of adult males in most villages between the elections of 1766 and the French census of 1771.

After the defeat, however, the well-known politics of families and factions took over once again (Gregory 1985). It was to dominate Corsican local politics to the present day and earn the island the reputation of being governed by tradition, if not by outright scoundrelism.

THE UNITY OF DUAL HISTORIES

The Western Mediterranean has fostered great empires, expanding states with centralized governments, societies with changing norms, urbanization, and even a certain economic development.[18] Parallel with the incessant creation of centralized political systems, seditious movements[19] with egalitarian and ascetic ideals have continually disturbed the peace. In modern times, disturbances in the area have been based on similar conflicts, the predominant one being between national, state-oriented ideals of progress, development, and justice and local structures inimical to central governments and ostensibly bent on preserving the social and political status quo.[20]

These two different social and political trends seem to correspond quite closely to generally accepted models of history-producing societies and traditional societies 'without history', respectively. The centralizing builders of expanding states view themselves as bearers of history, and their practice produces interrelated chains of events, logical changes, developments: a 'great history' proper. The egalitarian, exchange-oriented traditionalists view themselves as agents in local society, kin group, and neighbourhood, and their practice produces actions with limited effects and no structural changes, no development at all. Their practice is that of 'small histories', enacted within a framework of social, political, and cultural circumstances which their actions reproduce and secure as stable.

I have suggested here that when examined at close range the unruly and seditious local societies of the Western Mediterranean may be in no structural contradiction with the centralized states and expanding empires of the area. The mystery of the coexistence of two modes for society in this region might well be viewed as no mystery at all. It might be seen simply as a question of different articulations of the same system, the occasional merging of any number of 'small histories' into a greater one, combining separate structural principles in one practice with one focus. The equality found at the local level is a specific and very competitive form of equality, which takes as its starting point not the notion that 'any man is as good as I' but quite the contrary: 'I am as good as any man'.

The social practice enacting these values consists in an ongoing building up of power positions and their ever-recurring refutation by other position-builders. The seeming stability of traditional society is actually a *stable instability* which, seen from the inside, is a continually nerve-racking *history*, though small in comparison with those of empires or nations. Every family is an expanding political group, dreaming of power positions and overall control and gearing its marriage strategies, its economic activities, and its allocation of time, votes, and friendships to the superior goal of achieving political power. The competition of other, similar families is only one impediment and in certain contexts even an encouragement for any one family's ascendancy.

But what really keeps any one group from achieving total control of local society and expanding beyond it is the valorization of individual worth demonstrated in struggles over questions of honour (Knudsen 1990). Individual male honour generates conflicts which do not necessarily run along the lines drawn by political considerations; murders for the sake of honour may very well occur within political groups as well as within pretended 'families'. The violence accompanying honour values thus runs counter to power structures and constitutes a distinct, competing set of organizational structures. Appeasement is of no use where honour is concerned; only a resolute enforcement of justice and the effective prevention of any competing justice can merge the two systems of group formation into one and invest political structures with social values. That this can be done and traditional society thus be turned into an expanding, centralized state with a historical future has been demonstrated over and over in the Western Mediterranean. The structural affinity between these traditional societies and their history-producing variants does not of course explain *why* such events took place at any particular time or place. But recognition of this affinity will resolve the problem of stable structures in this type of traditional society by pointing to the fact that *structural stability* in this area is actually a *stable instability* with its own potentials for specific forms of change. By implication, this suggests that even our own history may not be the one-way street that modernity imagined.

NOTES

1 The earliest work to raise the question was White (1973). In Europe, the political relevance of the critique was first pointed to by

Glucksmann (1977), Baudrillard (1978), and Lévy (1977), who criticized *les grandes histoires* as not just arbitrary but oppressive. Among the abundant literature on the subject the most influential works apart from these have been Lyotard (1986), Perniola (1980), and Baudrillard (1983). These philosophers hold widely varying opinions but share an interest in the investigation of modernity's specific character and possible – even likely – end; hence the 'post-modern' condition in which people perceive themselves not as partaking in an ongoing 'great history' but merely as involved in local, 'small histories' which do not of necessity 'lead' anywhere. The European part of the debate is obviously influenced by Claude Lévi-Strauss, with his distinction between 'cold' and 'hot' societies, whereas White seems more inspired by German philosophy, notably Nietszche, Gadamer, and Luhmann. A common point of reference is Berger and Luckmann (1966).

2 And in concomitant literature; see, for example, de Saint-Victor (1882). Jeoffroy-Faggianelli (1979) has already drawn attention to this aspect of the scientific as well as other literature specifically regarding Corsica. Striking examples may be found in the introductions to Fée (1850), Marcaggi (1898), Valéry (1837), and Ortoli (1883), the last of which belongs to a series of which every volume conforms to the static picture of traditional society. The now classic critique of traditionalist images, the introduction to Hobsbawm and Ranger (1983), has had many followers. The static – or cyclical – image has spilled over into economic theories of development. For a well-informed critique of this effect, see Berger and Piore (1980).

3 Much as the obsession with feminine emotionality found in nineteenth-century literature provided the counter-image to a tacit valorization of supposed masculine rationality.

4 This of course is what in the eighties was described as the post-modern condition: a certain loss of direction which makes yesterday's evidences grotesque.

5 And sociological within the kind of sociology pursued by Marcel Mauss, Emile Durkheim, and, before them, the philosophers of *les lumières*.

6 This orientation, as originated by the *Annales* school, is in many contexts interesting, convincing, and necessary. I want to draw attention only to one of the questions which tends to disappear when it becomes dominant.

7 The original document is in Les fonds Paoli, série J, Les Archives départementales de la Corse du Sud, Ajaccio.

8 A single but extremely well-informed historical work treats the British attempts to rule Corsica of 1793–7: Gregory (1985) demonstrates with a wealth of detail how, in spite of rhetoric to the contrary, local power struggles impeded the 'enlightened' British rule of Sir Gilbert Elliot and finally made it impossible. See also Elliot (1874).

9 The peak of the century is found immediately after the autumn's municipal elections in the first year of the Second Republic (La 17ème legion de gendarmerie royale 1981). In a great number of

municipalities elections were marked by violence. An excellent analysis of nineteenth-century Corsican voting behaviour is found in Ravis-Giordani (1981).

10 Written and published by the canon Natali in 1736 under the interesting pseudonym of Curzio Tulliano Corso.

11 'Ainsi les statuts corses faisaient une distinction essentielle, ils tenaient compte de l'origine des biens pour en opérer la dévolution, les biens paternels ne pouvant être recueillis que par des parents paternels, les biens maternels retournant à la ligne maternelle' (Fontana 1905: 100).

12 The kinship ideology is so dominant as to be the exclusive explicit value system in both the eighteenth- and the nineteenth-century sources.

13 Elsewhere I have argued at length for the structural importance of a whole series of interconnected contradictions between professed values and actual practice in eighteenth- and nineteenth-century Corsican society (Knudsen 1987; 1988; 1990; 1991). Wilson (1989) notes that many vendettas actually took place *within* and not *between* families but does not seem to draw any analytical consequences from it with respect to either the Corsican self-representation as a 'kinship society' or the actual social organization which contradicts it.

14 'Quand l'une de ces nations formait un peuple roi, l'autre se croyait un peuple de rois; le pouvoir qui était collectif chez les uns, était individuel chez les autres' (Beaumont 1824: 19).

15 This evidently corresponds to Max Weber's (1968) famous phrasing 'monopolization of violence'. In my opinion, however, it is essential that violence be *meaningful*, that is, contextualized by social concepts, for this monopolization to assume state-building potential.

16 Cf., e.g., Soboul (1964) on the value system revealed by the Parisian *menu peuple* developing a national consciousness in the face of foreign threats and Cobb (1970) on the predominantly 'traditional' vocabulary in which patriotic (i.e., revolutionary) opinions were expressed.

17 The word 'nation' is in fact an anachronism in this context; the proper word is *patria*, which with its combination of feminine grammatical gender and masculine content expresses the contemporary attitude admirably.

18 The Roman Republic from the date of the conquest of Sicily in 241 B.C. created the first colonial system in this area, expropriating the lands of the conquered and deliberately changing their societies to suit Roman needs. In North Africa it took the Roman armies more than a century (107 B.C.-A.D. 21) to eliminate local (non-Carthaginian) political structures. North African mediaeval empires include, as the most impressive in the western area, the Rostemid (761–911), the Fatimid (910–1048), and the Almohad (1122–1248), all of which extended their power to the Iberian peninsula. For a general history of state formation in central North Africa, see Julien (1931) and Knudsen (1981).

19 Such as the sixth-century *circoncelliones* and eighth-to-tenth-century

kharedjites of North Africa and the twelfth-to-fourteenth-century *fraticelli* and similar movements of Italy and Corsica.

20 The 1962–4 conflict between the Algerian government and the warlords of the *wilaya* in the interior is a striking example, just as the Sicilian, Calabrian, and Corsican resistance to penetration by their respective national systems of politics and justice can only superficially be understood as a sign of generalized 'backwardness'. Throughout the area, questions of justice have been predominant, local communities practising vendetta and maintaining *omertà*, 'the code of silence', *vis-à-vis* centralized, formal justice.

REFERENCES

Arrighi, Paul (1966) *Histoire de la Corse*, Paris: Presses Universitaires de France.

Arrighi, Paul and Castellin, Philippe (1980) *Projets de constitution pour la Corse*, Ajaccio: La Marge.

—— (eds) (1983) *Disinganno intorno alla guerra di Corsica*, Ajaccio: La Marge.

Baudrillard, Jean (1978) *A l'ombre des majorités silencieuses, ou, La fin du social*, Fontenay-sous-Bois: Utopie.

—— (1983) *Les stratégies fatales*, Paris: Grasset.

Beaumont, Baron de (1824) *Observations sur la Corse*, Paris.

Berger, Peter L. and Luckmann, Thomas (1966) *The Social Construction of Reality*, Garden City: Doubleday.

Berger, Peter L. and M. J. Piore (1980) *Dualism and Discontinuity in Industrial Society*, Cambridge: Cambridge University Press.

Boswell, James (1768) *An Account of Corsica, the Journal of a Tour to That Island, and the Memoirs of Pascal Paoli*, London.

Carrington, Dorothy (1974) 'Pascal Paoli et sa "constitution" (1755–1769)', in *La Corse des lumières a la Révolution*, Annales historiques de la Révolution française, numero spécial corse, October-December.

—— (1983) *Sources de l'histoire de la Corse au Public Record Office de Londres, avec 38 lettres inédites de Pasquale Paoli*, Ajaccio: La Marge.

Cobb, Richard (1970) *The Police and the People: French Popular Protest 1789–1820*, Oxford: Clarendon Press.

Elliot, Emma Eleanor (ed.) (1874) *Life and Letters of Sir Gilbert Elliot, First Earl of Minto*, 3 vols, London.

Fée, A. L. A. (1850) *Voceri, chants populaires de la Corse*, Paris.

Fontana, Jean (1905) *Essai sur l'histoire du droit privé en Corse*, Paris.

Friedman, Jonathan (1983) 'Civilisational cycles and the history of primitivism', *Social Analysis* 14: 31–52.

Glucksmann, André (1977) *Les maîtres penseurs*, Paris: Grasset.

Gregorj, Gio. Carlo (1843) *Statuti civili e criminali di Corsica, pubblicati con additioni inedite e con una introduzione*, Lione.

Gregory, Desmond (1985) *The Ungovernable Rock: A History of the Anglo-Corsican Kingdom and Its Role in Britain's Mediterranean Strat-*

egy during the Revolutionary War (1793–1797), London and Cranbury, N.J.: Associated University Presses.

Hall, Thad E. (1971) *France and the Eighteenth-Century Corsican Question*, New York: New York University Press.

Hobsbawm, Eric and Ranger, Terence (eds) (1983) *The Invention of Tradition*, Cambridge: Cambridge University Press.

Jaussin, M. (1758) *Mémoires historiques, militaires et politiques sur les principaux événemens arrivés dans l'Isle y Royaume de Corse depuis le commencement de l'année 1736 jusques à la fin de l'année 1741*, 2 vols, Lausanne.

Jeoffroy-Faggianelli, P. (1979) *L'image de la Corse dans la littérature romantique française*, Paris: Presses Universitaires de France.

Julien, Charles-André (1931) *L'histoire de l'Afrique du Nord*, Paris: Payot.

Knudsen, Anne (1981) *Historiens Anden Scene: Historie i Periferien, Algeriet*, Copenhagen: IEA.

—— (1985) 'Internal unrest: Corsican vendetta, a structured catastrophe', *Folk* 27: 65–87.

—— (1987) 'Silent bodies and singing minds', *Folk* 29: 239–56.

—— (1988) 'Men killed for women's songs', *Culture and History* 3: 79–97.

—— (1989) *En Ø i Historien: Korsika, Historisk Antropologi 1730–1914*, Copenhagen: Basilisk.

—— (1990) 'Les idées muettes', *Etudes Corses* 20: 65–80.

—— (1991) 'Die Klarheit des Tötens', in H. U. Gumbrecht and K. L. Pfeiffer (eds) *Paradox*, Frankfurt: Suhrkamp.

—— (1991) 'Masculinity as challenge', in H. Bonde (ed.) *Mandekultur*, Copenhagen.

La 17ème légion de gendarmerie royale (1981) in *Mémorial des corses*, vol. 3, Ajaccio.

Lévy, Bernard-Henri (1977) *La barbarie à visage humain*, Paris: Grasset.

Lyotard, Jean-François (1986) *Le postmoderne expliqué aux enfants*, Paris: Galilee.

Marcaggi, J. B. (1898) *Les chants de la mort et la vendetta de la Corse*, Paris.

Marchini, Jean-Baptiste (1985) *Pasquale Paoli: Correspondance (1755–1769)*, Nice: Serre.

Mérimée, Prosper (1964 [1840]) *Colomba*, Paris: Le Livre de Poche.

Officier du régiment de Picardie [anonymous] (1889) 'Mémoires historiques sur la corse (1774–1777)', *Bulletin de la Société des Sciences Historiques et Naturelles de la Corse*.

Ortoli, Jean Baptiste Frédéric (1883) *Les contes populaires de d'île de la Corse*, Les litteratures populaires de toutes les nations vol. 16, Paris.

Paoli, Pasquale (1885 [1754]) 'Letter from Pasquale Paoli to his father, November 1754', *Bulletin de la Société des Sciences Historiques et Naturelles de la Corse*.

Pedersen, Poul (1985) 'Antropologiens evindelige krise', *Stofskifte: Tidsskrift for Antropologi* no. 12: 5–21.

Perniola, Mario (1983) *La società dei simulacri*, Bologna.

Petersen, Dorte Ulrik (1987–8) 'Maa-sai betyder: jeg vil ikke tigge!', *Stofskifte, Tidsskrift for Antropologi* no. 16: 89–100.

Pomponi, Francis (1971) 'Sentiment révolutionnaire et esprit de parti en Corse au temps de la révolution', in *Problèmes d'histoire de la Corse: Actes du Colloque d'Ajaccio, 29 octobre 1969*, Paris.

—— (1978) 'A la recherche d'un "invariant" historique: la structure clanique dans la société corse', in M. Caisson *et al.* (eds) *Pieve e Paesi*, Paris: Centre Nacional de la Recherche Scientifique.

—— (1979) *Histoire de la Corse*, Paris: Hachette.

—— (1981) 'Art et histoire', in C. Bonneton (ed.) *Encyclopédies regionales: Corse*, Artigues-près-Bordeaux.

Ravis-Giordani, Georges (1981) 'Ethnologie', in C. Bonneton (ed.) *Encyclopédies regionales: Corse*, Artigues-près-Bordeaux.

—— (1983) *Bergers corses: Les communautés villageoises du Niolo*, Aix-en-Provence: EDISUD.

Robiquet, M. F. (1835) *Recherches historiques et statistiques sur la Corse*, Paris and Rennes.

Rostini, Abbe (1881–2) 'Mémoires d'avant 1773', *Bulletin de la Société des Sciences Historiques et Naturelles de la Corse*.

Saint-Victor, Paul de (1882) *Hommes et dieux: Etudes d'histoire et de littérature*, Paris.

Soboul, Albert (1964) *The Parisian Sans-Culottes and the French Revolution 1793–1794*, trans. G. Lewis, Oxford: Clarendon Press.

Thornton, R. J. (1983) 'Narrative ethnography in Africa, 1850–1920: the creation and capture of an appropriate domain for anthropology', *Man*, n.s., 18: 502–20.

Valéry, M. [A. Pasquin] (1837) *Voyage en Corse, a l'île d'Elbe et en Sardaigne*, Paris.

Varnhagen von Ense, Graf (1894) 'Extrait des monuments biographiques du Varnhagen von Ense 1824–39', *Bulletin de la Société des Sciences Historiques et Naturelles de la Corse*.

Weber, Max (1968) *Economy and Society*, ed. G. Roth and C. Wittich, trans. E. Fischoff *et al.*, vol. 1, Totowa, NJ: Bedminster Press.

White, Hayden (1973) *Metahistory: The Historical Imagination in Nineteenth-Century Europe*, Baltimore: Johns Hopkins University Press.

Wilson, Stephen (1989) *Feuding, Conflict, and Banditry in Nineteenth-Century Corsica*, Cambridge: Cambridge University Press.

Chapter 6

Uchronia and the two histories of Iceland, 1400–1800

Kirsten Hastrup

One of the important lessons of historical anthropology is that modes of producing 'history' differ from one context to the next. Beyond the obvious differences in environment, economy, and social organization, the making of history is also in part determined by local ways of thinking about history. The conceptual and the material are simultaneous in experience of the world (cf. Ardener 1982; 1989a; Hastrup 1987; 1989a). This implies that there is more to time and causation than chronology and sequence. It also implies that a society may construe its history in a way unfamiliar to the Western historical genre.

These points have been extensively substantiated by the history of Iceland, which I have analysed in some depth (Hastrup 1985; 1990a; 1990b). This history displays a remarkable long-term oscillation between highly structured, well-organized autonomy and disintegration, dependence, and crisis. Paradoxically, these contrasting conditions seem to coexist with an equally remarkable conceptual continuity. Through the centuries there has been a conspicuous coherence and unity in the image of Icelandicness which – and this is the point – has had a decisive influence upon the course of history in this North Atlantic community. Obviously, part of the framework was already 'given'; we cannot and should not overlook the role played by such objective features as subarctic climatic conditions, geographical isolation, and political subjection. But even these features are subject to a particular local interpretation and a social response which transmutes objectivity into relativity. The irreversible is not the same as the inevitable, and the sequential is not coterminous with the causal.

Taking this as a point of departure, this chapter introduces the concept of 'Uchronia' as potentially useful for describing a particular way of thinking about history. As usual, the anthropological argument here has been spurred by a particular empirical history, that of the Icelandic society of the period 1400–1800.

TIME AND CAUSATION

Anthropologists have often portrayed other societies as timeless or 'without history', but this is unwarranted. All societies have histories of equal length and significance. If 'Europe' appears more historical than the rest of the world, as is implied by Wolf (1982), this is a *trompe l'oeil* owed to the fit between European history and its own conventions of representing 'history'. Similarly, peoples may have different concepts of time – as is abundantly demonstrated in anthropology – but as a species certainly share a fundamental sense of time (cf. Whitrow 1975; Bloch 1977). Phrased differently, societies may have different temporal registers and socially construct their histories in different ways (cf. Friedman 1985). In the words of Sahlins, cultural consciousness is objectified in a particular historical genre (cf. Sahlins 1985: 52).

In Europe, the cultural consciousness of history has been represented in terms of chronology and linear growth. This has shaped a particular way of thinking about causality. In general, causality is constructed upon past experience (Douglas 1975: 276). This means that it is an empirical matter. In human society notions of causality are based on local social experience and are part of a society's collective representations. Causality is identified in a context in which experience and definition merge and the individual and the collective are continuous with one another.

Thinking about history implies a conceptual organization of social processes in a meaningful sequence of events that are somehow logically and causally connected. It also implies a particular construction of social memory (Connerton 1989) and of cultural exaggeration and dialogue (Boon 1982; Borofsky 1987). I am not arguing that these kinds of historical thinking alone create history; there are of course certain identifiable events or social and political features that cannot be acquitted from influencing its course. I want to emphasize, however, that while we cannot separate the material from the conceptual, we must at least distinguish between the sequential and the causal. Causation in history cannot be identified without due reference to both events and internal ('cultural') patterns. The anthropological perspective on history thus adds a spatial dimension to the 'temporal causation' of historians (cf. Rabb 1982: 331).

In Western thinking about history, the context has been established as one of chronology. Events have been causally connected in time rather than in space. The latter would link particular events to culture and cosmology. Given the *post eventum* character of historiography (Leff 1969: 26), causal connections are established from events to antecedent phenomena – whence 'temporal causation'. The result is that antecedents in general have been treated as causes, opening the way for a process of infinite regress through chronological time. This process has, however, been punctuated, and *the* relevant antecedent has been selected. In other words, historians have tended to elevate their own representations of causality to a general theory of causation. 'Causes' have been identified quite arbitrarily as a matter of course. In an illustrative example, Marc Bloch shows how 'causes' are isolated from all the necessary antecedents not by their being the most necessary but by their being the most recent, the least permanent, and the most exceptional in the general order of things; they also seem to be the antecedents that could most easily have been avoided (Bloch 1954: 191). The explanatory problem is not simply one of arbitrariness in the identification of the (empirical) cause; it is also that 'the most constant and general antecedents remain merely implicit' (p. 191).

The shortcomings of the idea of temporal causation arise from the fact that, as Evans-Pritchard (1964: 174) observed, history is not only a series of events but also the links between them. Such links are provided by culture as well as by chronology. If we accept that cultural order is virtual rather than empirical, the individual historical event is culture made manifest. In the words of Sahlins, culture is *potentia* rather than *presentia* (Sahlins 1985: 153). For all the shared human experience of time, the potential ways of registering it are culture-specific.

In general, awareness of the past and hence of history derives from two distinct experiences: antiquity and decay (Lowenthal 1985: 125). The first implies a sense of age, the latter a sense of material change. The two need not be equally represented in different societies. This point is pertinent in dealing with Icelandic history in the period 1400–1800, when it seems that Icelanders

were living between two histories, one marked by age, permanence, and authenticity and the other by decay, change, and
extraneousness. In the collective representations of Icelanders
these two histories were unconnected – the experience of decay
was not integrated into the cultural consciousness – and the
consequences of this were disastrous.

THE HISTORICAL BACKGROUND

If society is the institutional form of historical events (Sahlins
1985: xii), there is no way to analyse it outside history. We are
thus immediately faced with a problem that was already identified
by Evans-Pritchard: when dealing with a changing social system,
'do we then speak of a society at different points in time or do
we speak of [two] different societies?' (Evans-Pritchard 1964:
181). This problem is acute in the study of Icelandic society
through time.

   Iceland was settled in the late ninth and early tenth centuries
by Norsemen in a final wave of Viking migration (Foote and
Wilson 1980). The largest proportion of settlers came from western Norway; Swedes and Danes were also represented, as were
second- or third-generation Viking immigrants to the British
Isles. In 930, the community of settlers, by then probably num-
bering some 40,000, was transformed into a society of Icelanders.
The constitutive event was the creation of a code of Icelandic
law and the establishment of a 'people's assembly' (the *alþingi*).
The constitution was advanced for its time; it separated legisla-
tive and judicial bodies and was based on the principle of representative democracy (if one may be permitted the use of an
anachronistic term). This first society developed and flourished.
People converted to Christianity in the year 1000 by a communal
decision at the *alþingi*. Writing was soon introduced, and among
the first things to be written down were the laws, which had until
then been orally transmitted; the elected 'lawspeaker' personified
society's memory of itself. Soon there would also be a major
written literature; the Icelandic sagas have been declared the
only Nordic contribution to world literature (Hallberg 1974: 7)
and still capture the interest of modern readers. The written laws
and the sagas are the primary sources for early Icelandic history.
   From these sources one may reconstruct a coherent social and
semantic system (cf. Hastrup 1985). Its coherence is related to

the fact that the Icelanders created their world from scratch, so to speak. Arriving in a virgin territory with no prior definitions of access to land and no preconceived class structure, the settlers were 'set free' from their inherited notions. It is true that they were deeply embedded in the Nordic world; their language was still spoken all over Scandinavia. From the literature we get an image of proud and egalitarian farmers concerned with honour and personal integrity, statemanship, and poetry. Although history gradually undermined this image by introducing social inequality and a measure of violent political conflict, medieval Icelandic society remained coherent.

In 1262–4, not without strong external pressure, Icelanders swore allegiance to the king of Norway. By then the population had probably reached some 70,000, and the principal mode of livelihood was farming. In the following century fishing gained more prominence, and when in 1380 Norway and Iceland became part of the Danish realm, Icelandic society was rather more composite than in the past. Icelanders were to remain subjects to successive Danish kings until the twentieth century. While the rest of Europe embarked on the road towards modernity, Iceland remained on the margins of this particular history. The economy was archaic, and the social structure remained atomistic and centred around individual households, with no social division of labour beyond them.

The Icelandic world of the period 1400–1800 was quite different from the mediaeval one. It was a disintegrating social system in which only a minority were 'free' in the old sense of being landowners, in which kinship no longer mattered for the rank and file, and in which mass death from starvation was recurrent. The more or less permanent social and demographic crises took place in an environment which had not altered drastically and in an epoch in which, for instance, Norwegian society was growing and flourishing under very similar natural conditions.

The contrast between the free sedentary farming community of the High Middle Ages and the starving and to a large extent shifting populations of later centuries, concerned with little more than survival, is striking. If society is the empirically identifiable form of historical events, it is tempting to speak of the two historical periods as distinct societies. However, if culture is an implicational space beyond the observable, the Icelandic world is marked by a continuity owed in part to the overcommunication of mediaeval glory and virtue. Icelanders of the latter period seem to have lived in a world marked by incongruity between the cultural order as constituted in society and the lived experience of people (cf. Sahlins 1985: ix). We shall see how this incongruity was related to an increasing discrepancy between social experience and the collective representations of 'history'.

SOCIETY: CONTEMPORARY EXPERIENCE

A key example of the discrepancy between Icelanders' social experience and their collective representations is provided by the development of their modes of livelihood. There had always been two complementary modes of subsistence, farming and fishing; the sources are unanimous on this. In his general description of Iceland from 1350, Abbot Arngrímur Brandsson states that 'fish from the sea and milk from the cattle are everyman's food' (1858 [1350]: 161), and in Bishop Oddur Einarsson's extensive 'ethnography' of 1589 we read that 'after milk-produce and meat from the cattle, the greater part of the food of the Icelanders consists of fish' (Einarsson 1971 [1589]: 124). Skúli Magnússon, a renowned Enlightenment reformer of Iceland, is even more elaborate in his description from 1786: 'the Icelandic economy is founded on only two gifts of nature: cattle-breeding and fishing, holding out their hands towards one another, since the latter gets life and power from the former, which again is supported by the latter' (Magnússon 1944b [1786]: 37). The Icelandic annals provide additional evidence that both economic activities were vital. If failure occurred in one, hunger was likely; if both failed, the consequences were fatal. Each household was founded on the dual economic pattern that seems to have been one of the structures of *la longue durée*.

Although recognized as complementary at the level of consumption, farming and fishing as two distinct systems of production did not occupy equal positions in the minds of Icelanders. They were never simply alternative ways of making a living, because they held asymmetrical positions in the (social) system of classification. We shall see how this contributed to the misery of the Icelanders in the period under examination here.

The domestic unit had been based on farming ever since the first settlements. There was a fine balance to be maintained between arable and stock farming; grain was grown in the early period, but the main crop was the hay that was vital for the livestock. Grazing was adequate only from June to September; for the rest of the year, the animals had to be kept at the farmstead on stored hay. The balance between animal numbers and labour input in the fields was, therefore, a delicate one. Grain-growing was soon abandoned; it is mentioned for the last time in 1589 as a rare occurrence in a small corner of the island (Einarsson 1971 [1589]: 126). With it disappeared the plough. This means that in the period 1400–1800 farming was principally a matter of hay growing and animal husbandry at a simple level of technology.

Land rights were specified in detail. By contrast to the Norse communities of Viking Age Scandinavia in which most of them originated, Icelanders had no primordial privileges in relation to land. The traditional Nordic principle of allodial rights based on kinship had no meaning in the early settlers' community in virgin Iceland. Land was therefore originally privately owned and could be disposed of with certain minor restrictions. Gradually, as generational depth was regained, kinsmen regained some of their old pre-emptive rights at least to the main land of a particular farm. Outlying farms or lands could be more freely disposed of. Landowners could also lease land to tenants, who had equal civil rights, or to cotters, who had a more dependent status. The important thing was to secure the maximum yield in this arid country; if tillable land was not used for two successive years the owner forfeited it. Labour was therefore a major issue in Icelandic culture.

The land itself fell into three categories – infields, outfields, and commons. Closest to the farm was the tilled and manured infield (*tún*), upon which hay or, earlier, grain was grown. At some distance were privately owned meadows and other outfields, used for grazing. In the earlier period the outfields also comprised saeters; individual farms had outlying shielings to which part of the household and livestock moved in summer (Hastrup 1989b). Beyond the privately owned land were the commons (*almenningar*), to which everyone had access for supplementary summer grazing, hunting, and gathering. Most of the earmarked flocks of sheep were left on their own in the mountain commons during the summer.

At the time of the settlements Iceland was covered with a primary forest of low birch. Although only one-tenth of the

Icelandic soil was arable, land appeared abundant and rich to the Norsemen, who according to legend were allowed to claim as much land as they could encircle on horseback from sunrise to sunset. As population pressure increased, land became scarcer. Large tracts were laid waste partly through soil erosion due both to grazing and to the cutting down of the vulnerable primary forest for house construction and for fuel. Soon houses had to be almost entirely constructed from stone and turf, and animal dung replaced firewood. This in turn reduced the supply of manure, and the delicate balance between the number of people and animals, on the one hand, and the size of the manured fields, on the other, was under constant threat. As a consequence, Icelanders became more dependent on fish.

Fish had always been plentiful and provided an additional resource for the farming households. During the fourteenth century fishing became a necessity, and it was further encouraged by the new external markets. The Hanseatic League replaced Norway as Iceland's main trading partner, and a new market for dried fish opened up in Europe. The net result was an economic upswing. The old trading ports, which had been nothing but temporary landing places, turned into tiny villages, and a category of 'professional' fishermen emerged. While earlier there had been no specialist groups at all, the late fourteenth century witnessed an incipient division of labour between farmers and fishermen.

In 1404, fishermen (*fiskimenn*) appear in the documents for the first time and, significantly, also for the last. The Black Death had ravaged Iceland from 1402 to 1404, reducing the population by some 40 per cent (Bjarnadóttir 1986). Farm labour had become scarce, and therefore farm service was made compulsory in 1404, obliging fishermen and workers to settle on farms and work for landowners or be exiled (*Lovsamling for Island* 1853–9, vol. 1: 34–5). Thus, just as fishermen emerged as a distinct group they were subsumed under farming. This is one of the first hints of the conceptual asymmetry between farming and fishing in the local definition of Icelandicness. Fishing continued, of course, out of sheer necessity, but the fisherman was subsumed under the general category of servants (*vinnuhjú*), defined by his position within a household (*bú*) headed by a landowner or a well-to-do tenant on Church or Crown property.

Fishing rights were generally defined by land rights; the landowner and his household had exclusive rights to fish in the streams and lakes on their own land and offshore within a certain distance from the shore, the so-called *fiskhelgi* (*Jónsbók* 1904: 188 ff.). Beyond that, the sea was defined as commons (*almenningar*). Thus land rights were apparently always given conceptual priority.

This can be inferred also from the fact that farmhands engaging in seasonal fishing had to return for the hay harvest at the latest, quite irrespective of the catch. During the fifteenth century, when Icelanders still had a clear recollection of the potential surplus created by fishing, the local court passed one law after another designed to make fishing less attractive. Thus, fishing with more than one hook on the line was banned, explicitly because farmers feared that if returns increased fishing would be too attractive to their servants (*Alþingisbækur Íslands* 1912–82, vol. 1: 432–4; vol. 5: 122). Sinker lines were likewise banned, and the use of worms as bait was prohibited. It was not until 1699 that some of these restrictions were lifted, sinker lines with several hooks again being allowed but only during the 'season': outside this period they were prohibited because of their allegedly damaging effects on farming (*Lovsamling for Island* 1853–9, vol. 1: 564–7). By then Icelanders seem to have lost the motivation, however; a century later, in 1785, Magnússon noted that lines with just one hook reigned all but supreme, and he made a strong case for the reintroduction of sinker lines with up to thirty hooks, giving a detailed description of how to make them (Magnússon 1944a: 55–6). Generally, he complained about the conspicuous deterioration of Icelandic fishing (Magnússon 1944b).

The decline of fishing technology had a parallel in farming, where a collective loss of skills can also be documented. We have noted that the plough fell into disuse, and we can add that the fences separating the infields from the wilderness disintegrated. Fences were required to protect the precious infields against stray animals; the laws on fencing had always reflected farming interests, but the peasants nevertheless failed to keep up with the requirements. In the eighteenth century this became a major issue, Icelandic living conditions having by then reached rock-bottom. In 1776 an ordinance was issued by the Danish king demanding that Icelanders reconstruct their fences under both the threat of fines and the promise of rewards (*Lovsamling for Island* 1853–9, vol. 4: 278 ff.). Judging from later decrees it was not an easy task to convince them of the necessity of the restoration. It was even suggested that exemplary fences be built in all regions for the people to study (vol. 4: 426). The old technology had apparently been forgotten even though the material (stone) remained plentiful.

The collective loss of memory is witnessed also in the fact that, instead of being stored in barns as in medieval times, hay was just stacked outdoors, where it was subject to rather humid conditions. The result of these developments was a lesser yield from the scarce fields and greater vulnerability to even one 'bad' winter. We know from the Icelandic annals that at least one-fourth of the 400 years examined here must be classified as lean years, with famine and death (Finnsson 1970 [1796]).

In short, one of the salient features of Icelandic society in the period 1400–1800 was a failure to keep up with the implicit requirements of social reproduction. Failure to exploit the potential for fishing, allegedly to protect farming, entailed increasing material poverty. This was correlated with a remarkable degree of collective amnesia as far as local technological skills were concerned. The result was that Icelanders became increasingly the victims of forces beyond their control. In the collective social experience, conditions worsened because of external threats, climatic and other. People became fatalistic – again, according to their own concepts of fate.

Since the earliest times, Icelanders had entertained two notions of fate (Ström 1961: 200–4). One concept gave the individual a certain measure of life; it was impersonal in the sense that one's measure was more or less a matter of chance. The other was personal and amounted to an innate quality of 'fortune'. This was the *gæfa* of the individual, one's personal gift for exploiting or even avoiding one's larger destiny.

These two concepts of fate gave rise to a permanent dualism in the Icelandic view of the factors determining the course of life. The course taken by individual – and hence social – history was the outcome of the joint forces of externally determined fate and the individual power to subvert it. By the old notions of causality, the individual Icelander would have taken fate in his own hands and reclaimed his influence upon history. But the social experience of Icelanders no longer sustained these notions. As time wore on, their experience was one of increasing impotence in all the domains of the social; survival had replaced influence as the most important item on the agenda. The idea of human causation in history gave way to the idea that the causes of change were external and largely uncontrollable. The economy deteriorated; people were exploited by the merchants and subdued by the distant Danish king. The wild approached from all quarters as the fencing of Icelandic society disintegrated.

To understand how this could happen – since it is by no means an immediate consequence of material factors – we must look into the Icelandic way of thinking about history.

UCHRONIA: REALITY IN THE PAST TENSE

If the production of history is related to thinking about history, then it is important to explore local notions of change and tradition in Iceland.

First of all, no conceptual distinction was made between history and story. The notion of *saga* referred to anything that was 'said' as history; as such it contained its own claim to truth (Hastrup 1986). When the main corpus of Icelandic sagas was written in the twelfth and thirteenth centuries, their objective was to recount the history of Iceland. Although certainly literary products, they were perceived as history proper. This was true also for the reconstruction of the ninth- and tenth-century events and characters in the *Íslendingasögur*, 'stories of the Icelanders'. In these sagas the pre-Christian past of Icelandic society is recast in the shape of a *Freiheits-Mythos* (Weber 1981) celebrating the original 'free state' of Iceland. Again, the literary activity of the thirteenth century may in fact be seen as an attempt to raise local consciousness about Icelandic achievements in *terra nova* (Schier 1975). Freedom and the taking of new land are tokens of original Icelandicness.

One of the consequences of Iceland's particular conflation of story and history, on the one hand, and its peculiar atomistic social structure, on the other, is a remarkable conflation also of individual and collective history. As one scholar has observed,

> There is no sense of those impersonal forces, those nameless multitudes, that make history a different thing from biography in other lands. All history in Iceland shaped itself as biography or as drama, and there was no large crowd at the back of the stage.
>
> (Ker 1923: 315)

If the individual Icelander was unable to control his own fate during the 'dark' centuries, he was equally unable to influence the larger history of Icelandic society. Actual history originated in a space beyond control, while at the same time the Icelandic dream was recreated in an Icelandic Uchronia.

Uchronia is nowhere in time. If Utopia is a parallel universe, Uchronia is a separate history, a history, so to speak, out of time. Uchronic visions were part of Icelandic collective representations of the world, and as such they deeply influenced the response of the society to its own history.

With modernity, a vision of history as linear growth emerged in Europe; this was to remain the distinctive feature of the Western historical genre, as we have seen, and the (largely illusory) basis for the comparison between 'Europe and the people without history' (Wolf 1982). In contrast to the old view of a qualitatively defined time-space, the new chronology and linearity implied that any stage in history was temporary. These features also indirectly sustained the idea that history could not go absolutely wrong because it had its own directional logic. Iceland resisted modernity until recently, and the development of Icelandic society teaches us that the vision of history as linear growth was alien to it. Even in modern Europe this vision remained élitist for a long time and may actually still alienate the rank and file from history in more ways than one.

The conceptual discrepancy between two views of history, if not actually between two histories, makes room for uchronic imagination. Where this is found, and certainly where it achieves the proportions of the Icelandic case, it reveals a feeling of incapacity to influence actual history. It also points, however, to a failure on the part of the dominant historical discourse to incorporate the experience of ordinary people. The gap between the two histories leaves people in a void.

Lacking experience of a progressive history, Icelanders knew that history could go wrong; the degree of misery that it entailed locally had no logic. In the fight between fire and ice, or between 'hot' and 'cold' conditions of history, Icelanders retreated to an imaginary time when history was 'right'. This gave rise to uchronic visions which were at odds with contemporary social experiences. Uchronia had its own reality, of course, but from our point of view this reality was hypothetical.

We cannot ask the Icelanders of bygone centuries about their imaginations, but we can infer them from a whole range of historical evidence. As a vision of another time, Uchronia connects otherwise disconnected elements and adds a level of comprehension to our historical narrative. The history out of time entertained by the Icelanders was informed by their view of the past. The past was over, yet in narrative form it was continuously reproduced and invoked in search of meaning in the void between two histories.

The reproduction of the old images of Icelandicness consisted in the constant renewal of a strong literary tradition dating back to the Middle Ages. Young people learned to read from the old lawbook, and the saga literature was consumed through the institution known as *sagnaskemmtan* (saga entertainment), the reading aloud of the old stories as a general evening pastime on the farms (Pálsson 1962; Gíslason 1977). As we have seen, the individual farmsteads represented society in miniature; there was no distinction between élite and popular culture as elsewhere in Europe (Burke 1978), no urban populations set apart from the peasantry. Although mass literacy was not achieved until some time around 1800 (which is still relatively early by comparative European standards), there is strong evidence that on most farms at least one person could read (Guttormsson 1983). What is more, the stories of sagas also formed the core of the popular verses (*rímur*) that were orally transmitted for centuries. The old images were thus continually reproduced by a recasting of the old myths of creation and of the past virtues of men. Through this recasting, the Icelanders were perpetually confronted with an ideal order nowhere in time. One could even argue that while other peoples have invented traditions to match new historical situations (Hobsbawm and Ranger 1983), Icelanders reproduced the images of the past to invent themselves.

The uchronic imagination was concurrently sustained by this invocation of the past. Because Icelanders had no 'real' others to identify 'themselves' against, the mirror-image of themselves in the past tense had major social repercussions. Living in the imaginary world of Uchronia, Icelanders had no symbolic exchange with others and no way of achieving a position from which they could see themselves and their situation in realistic terms. Because of their virtual isolation in the North Atlantic, they lacked a contemporary comparative reality against which they could measure their own culture (cf. Boon 1982). Paradoxically, this meant that the present escaped them; they felt this and clung even more firmly to Uchronia, which at least preserved a sense of injustice in the existing world.

Icelanders lived between an empirical and experienced history of decline and decay and an imagined Uchronia implying permanence and antiquity. Rather than defining a new reality and shaping it in language, they defined the present in terms of a past of which only the language remained real. Reality itself was discarded as anomalous because it no longer fitted the old language. Whatever creative skills the people possessed were directed towards a recollection and a continuation of 'proper' history – as story – at the expense of a comprehension of contemporary realities. Uchronia represented a structured world nowhere in time which strongly contrasted with the experiential space. Uchronia was a dream about a primordial society and a timeless history in which man was fully human.

CULTURE: ECCENTRICITY

Culture is the implicational space which gives meaning to social experience, and it was Icelandic culture in the period 1400–1800 that gave consistency to the disparate realities of society and Uchronia.

The disintegrating fences around the infields provide an apt metaphor for the developments of this period. Nature encroached relentlessly, diminishing the socially controlled space. The cosmological centre had always been locally represented by the household, which was society writ small and concretized in the landscape. In the classical period, a concentric cosmological dualism firmly distinguished between an 'inside' and an 'outside' world (Hastrup 1985). Inside, humans were in control; outside the wild forces reigned. As time wore on, more and more humans were alienated from the centre and merged with the wild because of poverty, vagrancy, or fishing. An increasing proportion of reality was beyond control.

'History' itself was split in two: an externally induced and uncontrolled succession of changes and an internally emphasized repetition of traditional values. The repetition owed its force to the reproduction of past images in a discourse which mirrored the negativities inherent in the contemporary Icelandic world. Lacking symbolic exchange with real others, Icelanders could engage in no relationship of identification other than with themselves in the past tense. In a manner of speaking, they became 'others' themselves. As such they were alienated from the larger history and ultimately from their own present.

This alienation was correlated with a particular pattern of event registration. Events are happenings which are registered as significant according to a particular cultural scheme (Sahlins 1985: xiv). This scheme is constantly placed at risk by social action; even social reproduction may eventually entail transformation (Sahlins 1981). But in Iceland the scheme persisted. The uchronic vision was intimately linked to the reproduction of the past in voice and in action. The literary image of the free farmer was proudly read aloud and was confirmed in action by the *alþingi*'s decision to concentrate energy on the reproduction of the farming households at the expense of fishing, among other things. Because of the reproduction of an outdated cultural scheme, actions became anachronistic, and contemporary happenings failed to register as events. In contrast to the event-richness of the past – as collectively memorized in the history conventionalized in the local genre – the present appeared event-poor (cf. Ardener 1989b).

Some social spaces or periods seem to generate more social events than others. This is not primarily a mensurational feature but a feature of registration. For events to be registered as such, they have to be significant from the point of view of the world as defining. The Icelandic world of our period did not single out many happenings as socially significant. The social space was event-poor; movement, change, and innovation were relegated to a non-social space in which no events were registered. While Icelanders certainly *had* a history during these event-poor centuries, they only indirectly *produced* it. Poverty was both material and symbolic; the two levels merged in the experience of the people.

Event-richness is a feature of space, and it is identified in the synchronic dimension. In the diachronic dimension, relative event-richness is transformed into relative historical density (Ardener 1989b). In the representation of history, historical density is a measure of the relative memorability of particular events. For events to be memorized and to become part of 'history' they must have been experienced as culturally significant. This apparently self-evident point covers a fundamental truth: the structuring of history and the selective memory are not solely imposed retrospectively. Contemporary event registration always serves as the baseline for the trace of experience left in history.

For Iceland this implies that the event-richness of the Middle Ages was matched by a historical density that contrasted with the unmarked reality of the later period. The continuous attention paid to past events made the present seem insignificant. The comparative historical density of the past also made the present seem not history at all. The reproduction of culture impeded the production of history. Inadvertently, Icelanders themselves contributed to the destructive course of developments. 'History' had become 'myth' and therefore beyond influence. What we are witnessing here, in fact, may be read as yet another instance of the inherent antipathy between history and systems of classification (Lévi-Strauss 1966: 232).

The dictum that culture encompasses the existentially unique in the conceptually familiar (Sahlins 1985: 146) had a particular truth in Iceland. The strength of the conceptual scheme actually entailed a failure to register the uniqueness of contemporary existential conditions. In other words, while 'culture' is an organization of current situations in terms of the past (p. 155), in Iceland the 'current situation' hardly registered because the 'terms of the past' were so vigorous. Having lost control of their own social reproduction, people were left without a proper historical appreciation of their main cultural categories. The unreflexive mastery of the traditional cultural system made the Icelandic habitus the basis for an intentionless invention of regulated improvisation quite out of time (cf. Bourdieu 1977: 79; cf. Sahlins 1985: 51).

The strength of the traditional language entrapped Icelanders in a state of refracted vision. Their world view was focused on another time, another history. Their culture became increasingly eccentric because of their uchronic vision, and this cultural eccentricity was instrumental in producing permanent crisis in Icelandic society. This particular way of thinking about history influenced its actual course; causation in history conflates the material and the conceptual, as does social experience.

REFERENCES CITED

Alþingisbækur Íslands (1912–82), 15 vols., Reykjavík: Sögufélagið.

Ardener, Edwin (1982) 'Social anthropology, language, and reality', in David Parkin (ed.) *Semantic Anthropology*, ASA Monograph 22, London: Academic Press.

—— (1989a) *The Voice of Prophecy and Other Essays*, ed. Malcolm Chapman, Oxford: Blackwell.

—— (1989b) 'The construction of history: "vestiges of creation" ', in E. Tonkin, M. McDonald, and M. Chapman (eds) *History and Ethnicity*, ASA Monograph 27, London: Routledge.

Bjarnadóttir, Kristín (1986) 'Drepsóttir á 15.öld', *Sagnir* 7: 57–64.

Bloch, Marc (1954) *The Historian's Craft*, Manchester: Manchester University Press.

Bloch, Maurice (1977) 'The past and the present in the present', *Man*, n.s., 12: 278–92.

Boon, James A. (1982) *Other Tribes, Other Scribes*, Cambridge: Cambridge University Press.

Borofsky, Robert (1987) *Making History: Pukapukan and Anthropological Constructions of Knowledge*, Cambridge: Cambridge University Press.

Bourdieu, Pierre (1977) *Outline of a Theory of Practice*, Cambridge: Cambridge University Press.

Brandsson, Armgrímur (1858 [1350]) *Guðmundur sage*, vol. 3, *Biskupa sögur*, ed. Finnur Jónsson, Copenhagen: Hið íslenzka bókmenntafélag.

Burke, Peter (1978) *Popular Culture in Early Modern Europe*, London: Temple Smith.

Connerton, Paul (1989) *How Societies Remember*, Cambridge: Cambridge University Press.

Douglas, Mary (1975) 'Self-evidence', in *Implicit Meanings: Essays in Anthropology by Mary Douglas*, London: Routledge and Kegan Paul.

Einarsson, Oddur (1971 [1589]) *Íslandslýsing: Qualiscunque descriptio Islandiae*, trans. S. Pálsson, introd. J. Benediktsson and S. Þorarinsson, Reykjavík: Bókútgafa menningarsjóðs.

Evans-Pritchard, E. E. (1964) *Social Anthropology and Other Essays*, New York: Free Press.

Finnsson, Hannes (1970 [1796]) *Mannfækkun af hallærum*, ed. J. Eyþórsson and J. Nordal, Rit Lærdomslistafélagsins, Reykjavík: Almenna bókfélagið.

Foote, Peter and Wilson, David (1980) *The Viking Achievement*, London: Sidgwick and Jackson.

Friedman, Jonathan (1985) 'Our time, their time, world time: the transformation of temporal modes', *Ethnos* 50: 168–83.

Gíslason, Magnús (1977) *Kvällsvaka: En isländsk kulturtradition belyst genom bondebefolkningens vardagsliv och miljö under senare hälften av 1800-talet och början av 1900-talet*, Uppsala: Acta Universitatis Upsaliensis.

Guttormsson, Loftur (1983) *Bernska, ungdómur og uppeldi á Einveldi-söld*, Reykjavík: Ritsafn Sagnfræðistofnunar.

Hallberg, Peter (1974) *De islandske sagaer*, Copenhagen: Gyldendal.

Hastrup, Kirsten (1985) *Culture and History in Medieval Iceland: An Anthropological Analysis of Structure and Change*, Oxford: Clarendon Press.

—— (1986) 'Text and context: continuity and change in medieval Icelandic history as "said" and "laid down" ', in E. Vestergård (ed.) *Continuity and Change: A symposium*, Odense: Odense University Press.

—— (1987) 'The reality of anthropology', *Ethnos* 52: 287–300.

—— (1989a) 'The prophetic condition', in E. Ardener, *The Voice of Prophecy and Other Essays*, ed. Malcolm Chapman, Oxford: Blackwell.

—— (1989b) 'Saeters in Iceland 900–1600: an anthropological analysis of economy and cosmology', *Acta Borealia* 6: 72–85.

—— (1990a) *Nature and Policy in Iceland 1400–1800: An Anthropological Analysis of History and Mentality*, Oxford: Clarendon Press.

—— (1990b) *Island of Anthropology: Studies in Icelandic Past and Present*, Odense: Odense University Press.

Hobsbawm, Eric and Ranger, Terence (eds) (1983) *The Invention of Tradition*, Cambridge: Cambridge University Press.

Jónsbók: Kong Magnus Hakonssons Lovbog for Island, Vedtaget på Altinget 1281 (1904) ed. Ólafur Halldórsson, Copenhagen: S.L. Møllers Bogtrykkeri.

Ker, W. P. (1923) *The Dark Ages*, Edinburgh and London: William Blackwood.

Lévi-Strauss, Claude (1966) *The Savage Mind*, London: Weidenfeld and Nicolson.

Leff, Gordon (1969) *History and Social Theory*, London: Merlin Press.

Lovsamling for Island (1853–9) ed. O. Stephensen and J. Sigurðsson, 20 vols., Copenhagen: Höst og søn.

Lowenthal, David (1985) *The Past Is a Foreign Country*, Cambridge: Cambridge University Press.

Magnússon, Skúli (1944a [1785]) *Beskrivelse af Gullbringu og Kjósar sýslur*, ed. J. Helgason, Copenhagen: Munksgård.

—— (1944b [1786]) *Forsøg til en kort beskrivelse af Island*, ed. J. Helgason, Copenhagen: Munksgård.

Pálsson, Hermann (1962) *Sagnaskemmtan íslendinga*, Reykjavík: Mál og menning.

Rabb, Theodore K. (1982) 'Coherence, synthesis, and quality in history', in T. K. Rabb and R. I. Rotberg (eds) *The New History: The 1980s and Beyond*, Princeton: Princeton University Press.

Sahlins, Marshall D. (1981) *Historical Metaphors and Mythical Realities*, Ann Arbor: University of Michigan Press.

—— (1985) *Islands of History*, Chicago: University of Chicago Press.

Schier, Kurt (1975) 'Iceland and the rise of literature in "Terra Nova": some comparative reflections', *Grípla* 1: 168–81.

Ström, Folke (1961) *Nordisk Hedendom: Tro och Sed i förkristen Tid*, Lund: Akademiförlaget.

Weber, Gerd Wolfgang (1981) 'Irreligiösität und Heldenzeitalder: zum Mythencharakter der altisländischen Literatur', U. Dronke *et al.* (eds) *Speculum Norroenum: Norse Studies in Memory of Gabriel Turville-Petre*, Odense: Odense University Press.

Whitrow, G. J. (1975) *The Nature of Time*, Harmondsworth: Penguin.

Wolf, Eric (1982) *Europe and the People without History*, Berkeley: University of California Press.

Chapter 7

Reflections on 'making history'

Anton Blok

> *There are* lieux de mémoire, *sites of memory, because there are
> no longer* milieux de mémoire, *real environments of memory.*
> Pierre Nora, 'Between Memory and History'

The phrase 'making history' is not without its problems. First, it
carries voluntarist overtones. As Marx wrote in his *Eighteenth
Brumaire*, 'Men make their own history, but they do not make
it just as they please . . .'.[1] In historical anthropology no less than
anywhere else, we have to come to terms with the unintended
consequences of human interaction – history's many ironies – as
much as its unintended conditions, for underlying all intended
interactions of human beings is their unintended interdependence
(Elias 1969: 193; see also Ortner 1984: 157). Second, if 'making
history' stands for 'constructing', 'constituting', 'fashioning', or
simply 'writing' history, we have to be careful as well. The past
is more than a construction, and to the extent that it is a construction – or reconstruction or deconstruction – one has always to
specify whose construction and to delineate the constellations of
power: whose claims on the past obtain recognition and acceptance, by what means, and why? Rival factions compete for historical truth. We have official history versus unofficial history,
history versus memory, memory versus counter-memory. In fact,
as recent developments in Rumania and the Soviet Union illustrate, we have representations and fashionings of different kinds
of memory, including dynastic memory and monarchical
memory, national memory and popular memory (Nora 1989).[2]

Some of these issues are addressed in most of the chapters of
this volume. Hauschild and Pina-Cabral, for example, portray
the struggle of the clergy and the Church for control over popular

imagination and memory. Their accounts are of particular interest in that they explicitly discuss the role of memory and the continuity of popular collective representations – issues somewhat neglected in other contributions. There is obviously a direct link between memory and history – Mnemosyne, the Greek goddess of memory, figures as the mother of history. We learn of a Lucanian priest who tells people what to remember and what to forget. We also learn about the opportunities at his disposal for controlling this process. Similar connections occur at other levels of society when the state tells people what to commemorate and what not. Official Polish history could not say very much about the massacre of Polish officers in the forest near Katyn by the Soviets in 1940 'until a joint Polish-Soviet commission charged with filling in historical "blank spots" recently declared it to be history' (Davis and Starn 1989: 5).

Before saying more about history and memory in the study of the past, we should also recognize an ambiguity in the word 'history', which means both the past and stories about the past, representations and what is represented. Whereas German *Geschichte* refers to the past or lived history and *Historie* denotes the 'intellectual operation that renders it intelligible', Dutch and French also have only one word each for designating the past and the study of the past: *geschiedenis* and *histoire* (cf. Nora 1989: 8).[3] This prompts further reflections on the meaning of the expression 'making history' and on the subject of historical anthropology itself.

Historians who include cultural analysis in their research rarely fail to indicate the extent to which they have drawn on the ideas and approaches of anthropologists (for a recent overview see Hunt 1989). When anthropologists use the term 'historical anthropology' they often have other things in mind. In her fine volume on the history and culture of mediaeval Iceland, Kirsten Hastrup writes about this problem as follows:

> At a very general level, history may be incorporated into social anthropology in two different ways. One is through analysis of a particular body of historical material; the other consists in the recognition of the time perspective in the analysis of social systems.
>
> (Hastrup 1985: 1)

A similar position is taken by John Davis, who remarks that 'if we wish to incorporate history in our analysis and explanation of social activity, we must pay some attention to the ways in which people construe the past'. Obviously, historical anthropology is here envisaged not primarily as the sort of convergence between history and anthropology about which we have heard so much since the early 1970s. The ambiguity of the term 'history' still hovers over the heads of anthropologists, for whom 'history' primarily signifies the past (and representations of the past) but leaves little room for historiography.

Writing about the famous *rapprochement* between the two disciplines, the American sociologist-historian Charles Tilly argues that (social) historians have always been good at specifying what has to be explained. They have learned a great deal from anthropologists, especially when they have to explain human action, and their whole discipline has been transformed in the process (Tilly 1978: esp. 208–9; cf. Davis 1981). For anthropologists, writes Tilly, the situation is quite different:

> The influence of historical work – including that of the *Annales* – on anthropological practice has been slight. Few anthropologists know much history, fewer know much about historical research, and fewer still employ the historian's models, materials, or insights in their work. The flow of influence between anthropology and history, as practicing disciplines, has been largely one-way. Under these circumstances, to speak of convergences between the fields is an exaggeration. To speak of the influence of the *Annales* on this particular branch of the social sciences is wishful thinking.
>
> (Tilly 1978: 213)

This was written some time ago, but few contributors to this volume have drawn on historical scholarship, and those who have have done so rather selectively. For example, in writing on 'dual history' with regard to eighteenth- and nineteenth-century material on feuding in Corsica, Anne Knudsen originally managed to do without Stephen Wilson's (1988) massive treatise on the subject, and the historical anthropology in her contribution and most of the others seems primarily informed by insights from other anthropologists, the names of some of whom seem to be *de rigueur* in much of the contemporary anthropological literature. Presentation of these credentials leaves little room for historians, who mainly appear on the scene as providers of historical facts.

There are few if any references to the writings of Fernand Braudel, Peter Burke, Norbert Elias, Carlo Ginzburg, Jacques Le Goff, Pierre Nora, Keith Thomas, Jan Vansina, and Paul Veyne, who have asked new questions, provided new perspectives, and suggested new ways of reading and interpreting historical documents, including oral testimony. Nor do these contributions include any such experimental ventures in historical anthropology as the work of Richard Price (1983), who matches Saramaka memories with archival accounts in a simultaneous presentation of texts and commentaries. The situation is somewhat different in France, where anthropologists, ethnologists, folklorists, and historians have long worked closely together (for a recent example see Le Goff and Schmitt 1981; see also Segalen 1986 and, for earlier examples of comparative scholarship, Hertz on funerals, Van Gennep on rites of passage, and Mauss on reciprocity).

Most of the contributions do make clear that, in the study of the past, one cannot neglect (as has long been done) the various ways in which different groups have represented or constructed the past. But it would be impossible to consider these without exploring how time is conceptualized, represented, symbolized, and constructed by different groups. In a recent study of the Swedish bourgeoisie, Löfgren (1987, citing Thompson 1967) describes how, in the late nineteenth century, an abstract, standardized, and quantified notion of time emerged that gradually pervaded the routines and trivialities of everyday life. These new perceptions of time also helped to differentiate public and private domains. Another example is provided by a study of world view in two parishes in the Alto Minho of northern Portugal; here Pina-Cabral (1987) describes how the perception of time and attitudes towards time are closely interwoven with social space and social order. A more ambitious and innovative approach to the study of time and memory is set out by Friese (1991) on the basis of her fieldwork in a mining and agricultural town in Sicily's interior. Rich in ethnographic detail, this work is of major theoretical importance. Friese shows how time is socially constructed while also serving as a social frame of reference. Combining insights from several disciplines, she demonstrates how notions of time are connected with meaning, give colour and tone to social relations, and are interwoven with power, hierarchy, and economic dependencies.

The study of time and memory may hold special promise for historical anthropology. One of the challenges is to explore the interdependence between history and memory and to find out more about the way in which memory and perceptions of time are bound up with space. The French historian Pierre Nora has argued that the *lieux de mémoire*, the sites of memory, are *topoi*, that is, both places and topics, where memories converge, condense, conflict, and define relationships between past, present, and future. Nora reminds us that 'the *ars memoria* was founded on an inventory of memory places, *loci memoriae*' (Nora 1989: 25n). Whereas space helps to shape social time, as Evans-Pritchard (1940: 94–138) recognized long ago, family names may prove to be the real tools of memory, situating individuals in known time and space (see also Zonabend 1984: 142 and, for a discussion of the tomb as a symbol of continuity, Bloch and Parry 1982: esp. 34).

But a true historical anthropology should not confine itself to the exploration of local and everyday notions of time alone. The latter are shaped – and eroded – by larger networks of relationships and processes which may not always be directly visible like clocks and calendars but which must be identified for a fuller understanding of the ways in which everyday practices and rhythms have developed or collapsed over time.

As specialists in local knowledge and the study of peasant culture, anthropologists have special credentials for saying something about the resilience, continuity, survival, revival, or collapse of this 'quintessential repository of collective memory' (Nora), now rapidly disappearing under the impact of state formation, industrial growth, migration, and mass culture.[4] If collective memory is, indeed, so intimately bound up with identity and social space, it may perhaps throw some light on the revival of nationalisms that we are currently witnessing in Central and Eastern Europe, where overarching state structures which have constrained or tried to eradicate those collective memories in the name of 'history' are breaking down or in the process of transformation and rearrangement.

NOTES

1 This famous phrase is often misquoted. It runs as follows: 'Die Menschen machen ihre eigene Geschichte, aber sie machen sie nicht

aus freie Stücken, nicht unter selbstgewählten, sondern unter unmittelbar vorgefundenen, gegebenen und überlieferten Umständen. Die Tradition aller toten Geschlechter lastet wie ein Alp auf dem Gehirne der Lebenden'.

2 In this connection see also Veyne's (1984: 19) notion of 'non-events': 'The non-events are events not yet recognized as such – the history of territories, of mentalities, of madness, or of the search for security through the ages. So the non-events will be the historicity of which we are not conscious as such'.

3 On the equation of memory and history, Nora further observes that

this weakness of the language that has often been remarked still delivers a profound truth: the process that is carrying us forward and our representation of that process are of the same kind. If we were able to live within memory, we would not have needed to consecrate *lieux de mémoire* in its name.

(Nora 1989: 8)

4 In a recent interview (*De Volkskrant*, 13 September 1991), Michael Ignatieff remarked that virtually no one still lives in the house or the town in which he was born and grew up. This century has made migration and exile the norm rather than the exception. In the world of a century ago, people knew each other's circumstances and family. Today the only visible ties with the past are not much more than a collection of photographs which are rarely shown and which can be arranged and edited as one pleases (cf. Ignatieff 1987: 1–2).

REFERENCES

Bloch, Maurice, and Parry, Jonathan (1982) 'Introduction', in M. Bloch and J. Parry (eds) *Death and the Regeneration of Life*, Cambridge: Cambridge University Press.

Davis, Natalie Zemon (1981) 'Anthropology and history in the 1980s', *Journal of Interdisciplinary History* 12: 267–75.

Davis, Natalie Zemon, and Starn, Randolph (1989) 'Introduction', in N. Davis and R. Starn (eds) *Memory and Countermemory*, Representations 26: 1–6.

Elias, Norbert (1969) 'Sociology and psychiatry', in S. H. Foulkes and G. S. Prince (eds) *Psychiatry in a Changing Society*, London: Tavistock.

Evans-Pritchard, E. E. (1940) *The Nuer*, Oxford: Oxford University Press.

Friese, Heidrun (1991) 'Ordnungen der Zeit: Zur sozialen Konstitution von Temporalstrukturen in einem sizilianischen Ort', unpublished Ph.D. thesis, University of Amsterdam.

Hastrup, Kirsten (1985) *Culture and History in Medieval Iceland: An Anthropological Analysis of Structure and Change*, Oxford: Clarendon Press.

Hunt, Lynn (ed.) (1989) *The New Cultural History*, Berkeley and Los Angeles: University of California Press.

Ignatieff, Michael (1987) *The Russian Album: A Family Saga of Revolution, Civil War, and Exile*, London: Chatto and Windus.

Le Goff, Jacques, and Schmitt, Jean-Paul (eds) (1981) *Le charivari*, Paris: l'Ecole/The Hague: Mouton.

Löfgren, Orvar (1987) 'The time makers', in J. Frykman and O. Löfgren (eds) *Culture Builders: A Historical Anthropology of Middle-Class Life*, New Brunswick and London: Rutgers University Press.

Nora, Pierre (1989) 'Between memory and history: *les lieux de mémoire*', in N. Davis and R. Starn (eds) *Memory and Countermemory*, Representations 26: 7–25.

Ortner, Sherry (1984) 'Theory in anthropology since the sixties', *Comparative Studies in Society and History* 26: 126–66.

Pina-Cabral, João (1987) 'Paved roads and enchanted Mooresses: the perception of the past among the peasant population of the Alto Minho', *Man*, n.s., 22: 715–35.

Price, Richard (1983) *First-Time: The Historical Vision of an Afro-American People*, Baltimore and London: Johns Hopkins University Press.

Segalen, Martine (1986) 'Current trends in French ethnology', *Ethnologia Europaea* 16: 3–24.

Thompson, E. P. (1967) 'Time, work-discipline, and industrial capitalism', *Past & Present* 38: 56–97.

Tilly, Charles (1978) 'Anthropology, history, and the *Annales*', *Review* 1: 207–13.

Veyne, Paul (1984) *Writing History: Essay on Epistemology*, trans. M. Moore-Rinvolucri, Middletown: Wesleyan University Press.

Wilson, Stephen (1988) *Feuding, Conflict, and Banditry in Nineteenth-Century Corsica*, Cambridge: Cambridge University Press.

Zonabend, Françoise (1984) *The Enduring Memory: Time and History in a French Village*, trans. A. Forster, Manchester: Manchester University Press.

Name index

Subject index